·····crochet for kids

Sweaters for Infants, Girls, and Boys

D1230973

Ann E. Smith

The Taunton Press

The Taunton Press
Inspiration for hands-on living™

The Taunton Press, Inc., 63 South Main Street, PO Box 5506, Newtown, CT 06470-5506
e-mail: tp@taunton.com

Distributed by Publishers Group West

COVER DESIGN: Anne Marie Manca
INTERIOR DESIGN: Cathy Cassidy
LAYOUT ARTIST: Cathy Cassidy
ILLUSTRATOR: Rosalie Vaccaro
PHOTOGRAPHER: Jack Deutsch
COVER PHOTOGRAPHER: Jack Deutsch

LIBRARY OF CONGRESS CATALOGING-IN-PUBLICATION DATA
Smith, Ann Emery.
    Crochet for kids : sweaters for infants, girls, and boys / Ann E. Smith.
      p. cm.
    ISBN 1-56158-512-2
    1. Crocheting--Patterns. 2. Sweaters. 3. Children's clothing. I. Title.

TT825 . S647 2002
746.43'4--dc21   2002001029

Printed in the United States of America
10 9 8 7 6 5 4 3 2 1

For my parents, Wayne Elizabeth and Bob Emery

● ● ● ●

ACKNOWLEDGMENTS

My talented Minnesota stitchers, Joyce Nordstrom and Elizabeth Hengel,
created the garments in this book with ultra-care. Anne Reed from Maine poured
over the patterns, carefully culling out any visible errors. My husband, Dean,
who helped me plan the book, critiqued the designs and inspired the written copy.
And I would like to thank Melissa Leapman for encouraging me
to take on this project and for cheering me along during the process.

CONTENTS

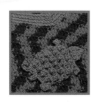

ABBREVIATIONS

approx	approximately
beg	begin(ning)
bpdc	back post double crochet
ch(s)	chain(s)
CC	contrasting color
cont	continu(e)(ing)
dc(s)	double crochet(s)
dc2tog	double crochet two together
dec	decreas(e)(ing)
est	establish(ed)
fpdc	front post double crochet
hdc	half double crochet
hdc2tog	half double crochet two together
inc	increas(e)(ing)
lp(s)	loop(s)
MB	make bobble
MC	main color
rem	remain(s)(ing)
rep	repeat(s)(ing)
rev sc	reverse single crochet
rnd(s)	round(s)
RS(s)	right side(s)
sc	single crochet
sc2tog	single crochet two together
sc3tog	single crochet three together
sl	slip
sl st(s)	slip stitch(es)
sk	skip(ping)
sp(s)	space(s)
st(s)	stitch(es)
tog	together
tr	treble crochet
WS(s)	wrong side(s)
yo	yarn over

INTRODUCTION

In tribute to the 1950s, this book is a journey through a kinder, gentler time:
A time when families left each summer for a two-week vacation, possibly to the beach.
A time when the children gathered around the radio on Saturday mornings to hear
"You better not go out in the woods today, because today's the day the teddy bears have
their picnic." A time when a TV western held the whole family captive for half
an hour on Sunday evenings. And, lest we forget, it was a time when gathering
school supplies and making school outfits filled the month of August.

TECHNIQUES

GETTING STARTED

- When purchasing yarn for your project, be sure to select skeins of yarn labeled with identical dye lot numbers.

- Before beginning any project, make a test swatch at least 4 in./10.2cm square. If the number of stitches and rows do not correspond to the recommended gauge, you must change your hook size. For fewer stitches to the inch, use a larger hook. For more stitches to the inch, use a smaller hook.

- Before beginning any project, read the instructions and underline all the numbers that apply to the size you will be crocheting.

- Be sure to read the "Before You Begin" notes and check out any variations, given in the "A Different Look" boxes.

READING PATTERNS

- *Work even* means to work in the pattern stitch as established without increasing or decreasing.

- *An asterisk (*)* indicates that the next portion of the directions should be worked once and then repeated. The text states the number of times to repeat: for example, "(sc, sk 1, sc) twice." It is also used to tell you how to finish a row; for example, "rep from * across."

- *A double asterisk (**)* indicates when to end the last repeat; for example, "rep from * across, ending last rep at **." When there is no double asterisk, crochet the entire last repeat.

- *Parentheses and brackets* are used to group directions. They enclose instructions that should be repeated a specific number of times: for example, "(2 sc in next sc, sc in next sc) twice." They are also used to set off and clarify a group of stitches that are to be worked as a unit: for example, "(2 dc, ch 1, 2 dc) in corner." Brackets are used with parentheses in some patterns; for example, "[sc, (ch 2, sc) in next st, sc] twice."

- *The front loop* is the loop that's toward you at the top of the stitch. The back loop is the loop that's away from you at the top of the stitch.

FINISHING UP

- For children's garments, join the sleeves to the body with crocheted slip stitches, and be sure to save some leftover yarn. Then, when the child's arms grow, you'll find it's easy to remove the sleeves and add a few more rows.

- When making the foundation chain at the lower edges of your garments, leave a long tail for sewing up the seams. Leave sewing tails at the shoulders as well.

- The careful assembly of your crocheted garments determines whether they look handmade or homemade. For professional seams, thread a tapestry needle with the same yarn as used in the project. With the right sides facing, take the needle and yarn through the first stitch on one side at the lower edge from back to front. Then bring the needle and yarn through the corresponding stitch on the other piece from back to front. Continue sewing in this manner for invisible seams. The technique is called mattress stitching.

TAKING CARE

- For stress-free laundering of your finished garments, first follow the yarn label instructions and test-wash your swatch.

- To machine launder your garment, turn it inside out and then wash on the delicate cycle.

- When giving a crochet project as a gift, be sure to include a yarn band. This provides the lucky recipient (or her parents!) with a handy laundering reference.

Down by the Sea

You can almost smell the sunscreen, hear the waves,
and feel the sand beneath your feet as you take a look
at the projects in this section. Sun, sea, turtles, starfish,
goldfish, and ducklings appear on blankets, sandals, hats,
and all sorts of wonderful sweaters.

Starfish Afghan

● ●

Take along this easy-to-launder afghan
so that little ones always have
a bright place to rest.

Intermediate

MATERIALS

- Red Heart Kids 100% acrylic (worsted weight), 5-oz./
  142g skeins (each 302 yd./276m): 1 skein Yellow
  #2230 (A), 2 skeins Blue #2845 (B), 2 skeins Lime
  #2652 (C), 3 skeins Turquoise #2850 (D)

- Size 6/G (4.25mm) aluminum crochet hook
  or size needed to obtain gauge

GAUGE

- First Star Motif = 5 in./12.7cm square

FINISHED MEASUREMENTS

- Length: 46 in./117cm

- Width: 36 in./91cm

ABBREVIATIONS

- fpdc = front post double crochet: yo, insert hook from
  front to back then to front to go around dc post
  (or fpdc), draw up lp, (yo and draw through 2 lps
  on hook) twice

- fpdc over fpdc = on RS, fpdc over fpdc 2 rows below,
  skipping sc behind new st; on WS, sc in top of fpdc

● ● ● ● ● ● ● ● ● ● ●

Before You Begin

- To change colors in single crochet: Draw up a loop with
  the current color; with the next color, complete the
  single crochet.

- To change color after a front post double crochet: With current color, work the front post double crochet until two loops remain on the hook; with the next color, yarn over and complete the stitch.

- When working with two colors in one round, carry the strand not in use loosely along the top of the last round and work over it as you go.

FIRST STAR MOTIF

With A, ch 4; join with sl st to form ring.

Rnd 1: Ch 3 (counts as dc), 14 dc in ring. Insert hook from front to back through third ch of beg ch-3 and draw up lp with B, yo and draw through 2 lps on hook—15 sts.

Rnd 2: With B, ch 1, sc in same ch as join and in next dc, changing to A. * With A, fpdc over next dc; change to B and sk dc behind fpdc. With B, sc in next 2 dc; rep from * around, ending fpdc over last dc; change to A and sk dc behind fpdc.

Rnd 3: Sk sl st; * with B, 2 sc in each of next 2 sc, fpdc over fpdc with A; rep from * around—25 sts.

Rnd 4: * With B, 2 sc in each of next 3 sc, sc in next sc, fpdc over fpdc with A; rep from * around—40 sts. Fasten off A.

Rnd 5: With B, sc in next st. * Hdc in next st, dc in next 2 sts, 3 tr in next st, dc in next 2 sts, hdc in next st, sc in each of next 3 sts. Rep from * around, ending sc in last 2 sc rather than last 3 sc—48 sts. Fasten off.

Rnd 6: With RS facing, join D with sl st in any center tr. Ch 1, (sc, ch 1, sc) in same tr as joining. * (Ch 2, sk 1 st, sc in next st) 5 times, ch 2, sk next tr **, (sc, ch 1, sc) in next center tr; rep from * around, ending last rep at **. Join last ch-2 with sl st in first sc. Fasten off.

Rnd 7: With RS facing, join C with sl st in any corner ch-1 sp. Ch 1, (sc, ch 1, sc) in same sp as joining. * (Ch 1, sc in skipped st from Rnd 5) to corner, ch 1 **, (sc, ch 1, sc) in corner ch-1 sp; rep from * around, ending last rep at **. Join with sl st in first sc. Fasten off.

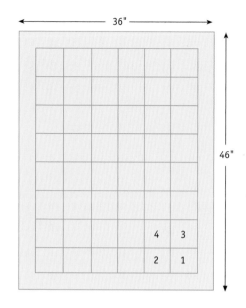

36"

46"

| 4 | 3 |
| 2 | 1 |

First Star Motif

Joining Second Star Motif

Joining Third Star Motif

Joining Fourth Star Motif

Rnd 8: With RS facing, join D with sl st in any corner ch-1 sp. Ch 1, (sc, ch 1, sc) in same sp as joining. * (Ch 2, sc in next ch-1 sp) to corner, ch 2 **, (sc, ch 1, sc) in corner ch-1 sp; rep from * around, ending last rep at **. Join with sl st in first sc. Fasten off.

SECOND STAR MOTIF
(joining one side)

Rnds 1–7: Same as for First Star Motif.

Rnd 8: With RS facing, join D with sl st in any corner ch-1 sp. Ch 1, (sc, ch 1, sc) in same sp as joining. * (Ch 2, sc in next ch-1 sp) to corner, ch 2 **, (sc, ch 1, sc) in corner ch-1 sp; rep from * to ** again.

[(Sc, ch 1) in corner ch-1 sp, drop st, insert hook into corresponding corner ch-1 sp of first star motif, (ch 1, sc) in same corner of second star motif—corner connection made]. (Ch 2, drop st, insert hook from front to back and into next ch-2 sp on first star motif, ch 2, sc in next ch-1 sp on second star motif—side connection made) 7 times. Ch 2, connect to ch-2 sp on first star motif, ch 2, (sc, ch 1) in second star motif corner, ch 1 and connect to first star motif corner sp, (ch 1, sc) in second star motif corner. (Ch 2, sc in next sp of second star motif) across, ending ch 2, sl st in first sc. Fasten off.

THIRD STAR MOTIF
(joining one side and a corner)

Rnds 1–7: Same as for First Star Motif.

Rnd 8: With RS facing, join D with sl st in any corner ch-1 sp. Ch 1, (sc, ch 1, sc) in same sp as joining. * (Ch 2, sc in next ch-1 sp) to corner, ch 2 **, (sc, ch 1, sc) in corner ch-1 sp; rep from * to ** again. (Sc, ch 1) in corner ch-1 sp, connect to corner ch-1 sp of second star motif, ch 1, sc in same corner sp on third star motif. (Ch 2, connect to next ch-2 sp on second star motif, ch 2, sc in next ch-2 sp on third star motif) 7 times. Ch 2, connect to ch-2 sp on second star motif, ch 2, (sc, ch 1) in corner ch-1 sp on third star motif, ch 1, connect to corner ch-1 sp on second star motif, ch 1, sc in same corner of third star motif. Working along third star motif side (ch 2, sc in next ch-1 sp) 7 times, ch 2, sl st in first sc. Fasten off.

FOURTH STAR MOTIF
(joining two sides)

Rnds 1–7: Same as for First Star Motif.

Rnd 8: With RS facing, join D with sl st in any corner ch-1 sp. Ch 1, (sc, ch 1, sc) in same sp as joining. * (Ch 2, sc in next ch-1 sp) to corner, ch 2, (sc, ch 1) in corner ch-1 sp, connect to third star motif corner sp, (ch 1, sc) in same corner sp on fourth star motif. (Ch 2, connect to next ch-2 sp on third star motif, ch 2, sc in next ch-1 sp on fourth star motif) 7 times, ch 2, connect in next ch-2 sp on third star motif, ch 2. (Sc, ch 1) in corner of fourth star motif, ch 1, connect to corner sp of third star motif, (ch 1, sc) in same corner of fourth star motif, ch 1, connect to corner sp of first star motif, (ch 1, sc) in same corner sp of fourth star motif. (Ch 2, connect to next ch-2 sp of first star motif, ch 2, sc in next ch-1 sp on fourth star motif) 7 times, ch 2, connect to next ch-2 sp on first star motif, ch 2, (sc, ch 1) in fourth star motif corner sp, connect to first star motif corner sp, (ch 1, sc) in same corner sp of fourth star motif. (Ch 2, sc in next ch-1 sp on fourth star motif) 7 times, ch 2, join with sl st in first sc. Fasten off.

Cont adding motifs, using joining methods as described, until piece is 6 motifs wide and 8 motifs high—48 total motifs.

A Different Look

For a deeper border, do not fasten off after Round 12. Instead of making a slip stitch in the same space as the joining, slip stitch in the next chain-2 space. Then continue working chain 2, slip stitch in the next space around and around until the border is as deep as you like it. Just be sure that you end in the same location as you began, so that all sides have the same number of rounds.

BORDER

Rnd 1: With RS facing, join C with sl st in any corner ch-1 sp. Ch 1, (sc, ch 1, sc) in same sp as joining. * (Ch 1, sc in next ch-2 sp) across, working (ch 1, sc in corner ch-1 sp, sk joining, ch 1, sc in next corner ch-1 sp), (ch 1, sc in next ch-2 sp) to corner, ch 1 **, (sc, ch 1, sc) in corner. Rep from * around, ending last rep at **. Join with a sl st in first sc and fasten off.

Rnd 2: With RS facing, join D with sl st in any corner ch-1 sp. Ch 1, (sc, ch 1, sc) in same sp as joining. * (Ch 2, sc in next ch-1 sp) to corner, ch 2 **, (sc, ch 1, sc) in corner ch-1 sp; rep from * around, ending last rep at **. Join with sl st in first sc and fasten off.

Rnds 3–11: Rep Rnds 1 to 2 for 4 times more, then rep Rnd 1 again.

Rnd 12: With RS facing, join D with sl st in any corner ch-1 sp. (Ch 2, sl st in next sp) around entire afghan, ending ch 2, sl st in same sp as joining. Fasten off.

Ahoy!

Vertical waves created with simple front post double crochet stitching give this jacket a soft texture. Bobbles and picots trim the sailor collar, sleeve cuffs, and lower edge. Whimsical lighthouse buttons and purchased rickrack add a delightful splash of color.

MATERIALS

Jacket

- Naturally Cotton Connection (DK weight; distributed by S. R. Kertzer), 1.75-oz./50g skeins (each 115 yd./105m): 6 (7, 8) skeins Natural No. 8

- Size 4/E (3.50mm) aluminum crochet hook **or size needed to obtain gauge**

- Size 5/F (4.00mm) aluminum crochet hook

- Tapestry needle

- JHB International Buttons, 1⅛ in./2.8cm long: 3 Beacon, #50921 (Red/Black/White)

- Wrights Baby Rick Rack, ¼-in./6mm wide, 1 package Red #065 and 1 package Blue #078

Tam

- 3 skeins Natural No. 8

- 1 button, Beacon #50921

- 1 package each Rick Rack: Red #605 and Blue #078

The Set

- 9 (10, 11) skeins Natural No. 8

- 4 buttons, Beacon #50921

- 1 package each Rick Rack: Red #605 and Blue #078

GAUGE

- In Body Pattern with smaller hook: 13 sts = 3 in./
  7.6cm; 18 rows = 4 in./10.2cm

SIZES
Jacket

- For wee ones, 12 (18, 24) months; directions are
  written for the smallest size with changes for
  the larger sizes in parentheses

Tam

- One size

FINISHED MEASUREMENTS
Jacket

- Chest (buttoned): 21¼ (25¼, 29) in./
  53.4 (64.1, 73.7)cm

- Length: 14 (15, 16) in./35.6 (38.1, 40.6)cm

Tam

- Band (circumference): 19 in./48.3cm

ABBREVIATIONS

- fpdc = front post double crochet: yo, insert hook from
  front to back then to front to go around dc post, draw
  up lp, (yo and draw through 2 lps on hook) twice

- fpdc over fpdc = on RS, fpdc over fpdc 2 rows below,
  skipping sc behind new st; on WS, sc in top of fpdc

- sc2tog = draw up lp in each of next 2 sts, yo and draw
  through all 3 lps on hook

●●●●●●●○○○○

Before You Begin

- Note that the borders are added after the garment has
  been sewn together.

- Turn at the end of each row.

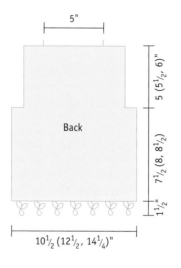

Back

5"

5 (5½, 6)"

7½ (8, 8½)"

1½"

10½ (12½, 14¼)"

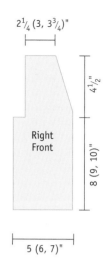

Right
Front

2¼ (3, 3¾)"

4½"

8 (9, 10)"

5 (6, 7)"

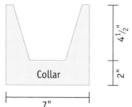

Collar

4½"

2"

7"

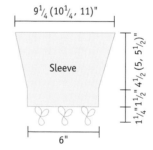

Sleeve

9¼ (10¼, 11)"

4½" (5, 5½)"

1¼" 1½" 4½"

6"

PATTERN STITCHES
Body Pattern

multiple of 4 sts + 2 sts; rep of 12 rows

Row 1 (RS): Ch 1; * sc in each of 3 sc, fpdc over fpdc;
rep from * across, ending sc in last 2 sc.

Row 2 and each WS row: Ch 1, sc in each sc and fpdc
across.

Row 3: Ch 1, sc in 2 sc; * fpdc over fpdc, sc in 3 sc; rep
from * across.

Row 5: Ch 1, sc in sc; * fpdc over fpdc, sc in 3 sc; rep
from * across, ending fpdc over fpdc, sc in last 4 sc.

Row 7: Rep Row 3.

Row 9: Rep Row 1.

Row 11: Ch 1, sc in first 4 sc; * fpdc over fpdc, sc in 3 sc; rep from * across, ending fpdc over fpdc, sc in last 1 sc.

Row 12: Ch 1, sc in each sc and fpdc across.

Rep Rows 1 to 12 for Body Pattern.

Puff Stitch

In next st (yo and draw up a lp) 3 times, yo and draw through 6 lps on hook, yo and draw through 2 lps on hook.

Picots

In next st (sl st, ch 3, sl st, ch 5, sl st, ch 3, sl st).

• Jacket •

BACK

Beg at lower edge and with smaller hook, ch 48 (56, 64).

Foundation: Row 1 (RS): Dc in fourth ch from hook and in each ch across—46 (54, 62) sts.

Row 2: Ch 1, sc in each dc across.

Row 3: Ch 1, sc in first sc; (fpdc over next dc 2 rows below, sk sc behind fpdc, sc in next sc) across, ending sc in last sc.

Row 4: Ch 1, sc in each sc and fpdc across.

Row 5: Ch 1, sc in each of first 3 sc; (fpdc over fpdc, sc in next 3 sc) across, ending fpdc over fpdc, sc in last 2 sc.

Row 6: Ch 1, sc in each sc and fpdc across.

Rep Body Pattern to approx 7½ (8, 8½) in./19.1 (20.3, 21.6)cm from beg, ending with WS row. Fasten off.

Armhole Shaping: With RS facing, join yarn with sl st in fifth st from right edge. Ch 1, cont in est pattern across, leaving last 4 sts unworked—38 (46, 54) sts.

Cont pattern to approx 12½ (13½, 14½) in./31.8 (34.3, 36.9)cm from beg, ending with RS row. Fasten off.

LEFT FRONT

Beg at lower edge and with smaller hook, ch 24 (28, 32). Rep Foundation Rows 1 to 6 as for Back—22 (26, 30) sts. Work in Body Pattern to approx 7½ (8, 8½) in./ 19.1 (20.3, 21.6)cm from beg, ending with WS row. Fasten off.

Armhole Shaping: With RS facing, join yarn with sl st in fifth st from right edge. Ch 1, cont est pattern across 18 (22, 26) sts. Work even to approx 8 (9, 10) in./ 20.3 (22.9, 25.4)cm from beg, ending with WS row.

Neck Shaping: Work est pattern across, leaving last st unworked. Dec 1 st at neck edge on this row and then every other row 6 (7, 8) times more. Work even on rem 10 (13, 16) sts to same length as Back. Fasten off.

RIGHT FRONT

Work as for Left Front through completion of Foundation Row 2.

Row 3: Ch 1, sc in 2 sc; (fpdc over next dc two rows below, sk sc behind fpdc, sc in next sc) across.

Row 4: Ch 1, sc in each sc and fpdc across.

Row 5: Ch 1, sc in 2 sc; (fpdc over fpdc, sc in next 3 sc).

Row 6: Rep Row 4.

Beg Body Pattern with Row 1 and cont as est to approx 7½ (8, 8½) in./19.1 (20.3, 21.6)cm from beg, ending with WS row.

Armhole Shaping: Cont in pattern across, leaving last 4 sts unworked. Work even to approx 8 (9, 10) in./ 20.3 (22.9, 25.4)cm from beg, ending with WS row.

Neck Shaping: Sl st in first sc and cont in pattern across. Sc across, ending sc2tog. Cont in pattern, dec

1 st at neck edge every other row 6 (7, 8) times more. Complete as for Left Front.

SLEEVES (make two)

Beg at lower edge and with smaller hook, ch 28. Work Foundation Rows 1 to 6 as for Back—26 sts. Beg Body Pattern and work to approx 1½ in./3.8cm) from beg. Cont in est pattern, inc 1 st each edge every other row 7 (9, 11) times—40 (44, 48) sts. Work even to approx 6 (6½, 7) in./15.2 (16.5, 17.8)cm from beg, ending with RS row. Fasten off.

COLLAR

Beg at back and with smaller hook, ch 32. Rep Foundation Rows 1 to 2 as for Back—30 sts.

Row 3: Ch 1, sc in first 3 sc; (fpdc in dc two rows below, sk sc behind fpdc, sc in next 3 sc) across, ending fpdc in dc two rows below, sk sc behind fpdc, sc in last 2 sc.

Row 4: Ch 1, sc in each sc and fpdc across.

Work Rows 3 to 7 of Body Pattern.

Neck Shaping: Ch 1, sc in each of first 7 sts; turn. Cont as est, dec 1 st at neck edge every fourth row 4 times. Work even on the 3 sts to approx 6½ in./16.5cm from beg, ending with RS row. Fasten off. With WS facing, sk center 16 sts, join yarn with sl st in next st. Ch 1, sc in same st as joining and in each of next 6 sts. Work this side as est.

FINISHING

Join shoulder seams. Set in sleeves, sewing side edges to skippped armhole sts for square armholes. Join underarm and side seams.

Sleeve Border (make two)
With RS facing and smaller hook, join yarn with sl st near seam. Ch 1, work 25 sc evenly spaced around; join and turn.

Rnd 2: Ch 1, sc in 2 sc; (Puff Stitch in next st, sc in next 3 sts) around, ending Puff Stitch in next st, sc in 2 sc; join and turn.

Rnd 3: Ch 1, sl st in 2 sc; (Picots in Puff Stitch, sl st in next 3 sc) around, ending Picots in Puff Stitch, sl st in last 2 sc. Fasten off.

Collar

Pin RS of collar to WS of garment so that lower edges of collar end at first V-neck shaping row. Sl st in place. With RS facing, join yarn at edge of left collar edge. Work 33 sc evenly spaced to corner, 2 sc in first sc at corner, work 28 sc along collar edge, 2 sc in corner, 33 sc evenly spaced to lower edge; turn.

Row 2: Ch 1, sc in 2 sc; (Puff Stitch in next sc, sc in next 3 sc) 8 times, Puff Stitch in next sc, sc in 2 sc, (Puff Stitch in next sc, sc in next 3 sc) 6 times, (Puff Stitch in next sc, sc in next 2 sc) twice, (Puff Stitch in next sc, sc in next 3 sc) 7 times, Puff Stitch in next sc, sc in 2 sc; turn.

Row 3: Ch 1, sl st in first 2 sc; working Picots in each Puff Stitch, sl st in sc around. Fasten off.

Right Front Band

With RS facing and smaller hook, join yarn in corner at lower edge. Ch 1, work 48 sl sts evenly spaced along edge; sl st in side of collar; turn.

Row 2: Ch 1, sk 1 sl st, sc in each of next 48 sl sts.

Row 3: Ch 1, sc in 17 sc; (ch 3, sk 3 sc, sc in each of next 10 sc) twice, ch 3, sk 3 sc, sc in each of next 2 sc; sl st in side of collar.

Row 4: Ch 1, sk the sl st, sc in each sc across, working 3 sc in each ch-3 sp.

Row 5: Ch 1, sl st in each sc across, ending sl st in Puff Stitch row of collar. Fasten off.

Left Front Band

With RS facing and smaller hook, join yarn at first neck shaping row near collar with sl st; make 47 more sl sts along edge.

Row 2: Ch 1, sc in each sl st across; sl st in side of collar.

Row 3: Ch 1, sk the sl st, sc in each sc across.

Row 4: Rep Row 2, making sl st in Puff Stitch row of collar.

Row 5: Ch 1, sk the sl st, sl st in each sc across and fasten off.

Sew buttons opposite buttonholes.

Lower Border

With RS facing and larger hook, join yarn at lower left front edge. Ch 1, work 3 sc across band, work 88 (104, 120) sc evenly spaced along edge and 3 sc across band—94 (110, 126) sts.

Row 2: With larger hook, ch 1. Sc in first 2 sc; (Puff Stitch in next sc, sc in next 3 sc) across.

Row 3: With smaller hook, ch 1, sl st in each sc across, working Picots in each Puff Stitch. Fasten off.

Embellishment: Thread blue and red rickrack into tapestry needle. In sleeve row before border, loosely weave trim over sc and under fpdc around. At end, tie into bow. Take red rickrack under first Puff Stitch on collar edge, then weave over sc sts and under Puff Stitches around; leaving a 4 in./10.2cm tail at each end, cut trim. Weave blue rickrack next to red; then weave one more piece of red rickrack; cut, leaving tails. Tie tails into overhand knot on each side.

• Tam •

BASE

With smaller hook, ch 140. Dc in fourth ch from hook and in each ch across—138 sts. Ch 1, sc in each dc across. Ch 1; * sc in 3 sc, fpdc over dc two rows below, sk sc behind fpdc; rep from * across, ending sc in 2 sc. Work Body Pattern Rows 2 to 12; then Rows 1 to 2. Join with sl st in first sc.

CROWN

Rnd 1: Sc in 3 sc; * fpdc over fpdc, sc in 3 sc, sk 1 sc, sc in 3 sc; rep from * around, ending fpdc over fpdc, (sc in 2 sc, sk 1 sc) twice—120 sts.

Rnd 2 and each even-numbered rnd: Sc in each sc and fpdc around.

Rnd 3: Sc in 2 sc; * sk 1 sc, fpdc over fpdc, sk sc behind fpdc and next sc, sc in 4 sc; rep from * around, ending sk 1 sc, fpdc over fpdc, sk sc behind fpdc and next sc, sc in 3 sc—86 sts.

Rnd 5: Sc in 2 sc; * fpdc over fpdc, sc in 4 sc; rep from * around, ending fpdc over fpdc, sc in 3 sc.

Rnd 7: Sc in 1 sc; * sk 1 sc, fpdc over fpdc, sk sc behind fpdc and next sc, sc in 2 sc; rep from * around—52 sts.

Rnd 9: Sc in sc; * fpdc over fpdc, sc in 2 sc; rep from * around.

Rnd 11: * Fpdc over fpdc, sc2tog; rep from * around, ending sc2tog over last and first sc—34 sts.

Rnd 13: * Fpdc over fpdc, sc in sc; rep from * around.

Rnd 15: Fpdc in each fpdc around—17 sts.

Rnd 16: Sc in each fpdc around.

Rnd 17: Rep Rnd 15.

Rnd 18: (Sc in fpdc, sk next fpdc) around, ending sc in fpdc—9 sts.

Rnd 19: * Sl st in sc, ch 15, (sl st in second ch from hook, Puff Stitch in next ch) across, ending sl st in last ch and in same sc as beg ch; rep from * around. Fasten off, leaving a tail. Take tail to inside and use to close opening.

BAND

With RS facing and smaller hook, join with sl st at lower edge. Ch 1, sc in same st as join; (sk next st, sc in next st) across, ending sk last sc—69 sts; join with sl st in first sc; turn.

Row 2: Ch 1, sc2tog, sc in next sc; (Puff Stitch in next sc, sc in next 3 sc) across, ending Puff Stitch in next sc, sc in next sc—68 sts; join and turn.

Row 3: Ch 1, sc in each sc and Puff Stitch across; join and turn.

Row 4: Ch 1; (Puff Stitch in next sc, sc in next 3 sc) across; join and turn.

Row 5: Rep Row 3.

Row 6: Ch 1, sc in 2 sc; (Puff Stitch in next sc, sc in next 3 sc) across, ending Puff Stitch in next sc, sc in last sc; join and turn.

Row 7: In first sc (sl st, ch 3, sl st); * sl st in next sc, in next sc (sl st, ch 3, sl st) rep from * around, ending sl st in last sc. Fasten off.

Join back seam. With blue and red rickrack, form a bow. Sew bow onto side of band; then sew button in center of bow.

Size It Right!

If the finished tam is a bit large for your wee one, weave elastic thread (available at fabric stores) along the wrong side of the band, pulling it up to fit.

Beach Treasures

●●●●●●●●●●●●●●●●●●●●●●●●●   ●●●●

Goldfish dangling from lines and big pink shells border this cute dress for a little girl. Made of washable cotton, the dress is perfect for warm days. And who could resist kissing the tiny toes that peak out of the bright sandals!

MATERIALS

Dress

● Lily Sugar 'n Cream cotton yarn (sport weight; distributed by Spinrite Inc.), 1.75-oz./50g balls (each 125 yd./114m): 3 (4, 5, 6, 8) balls Emerald #15 (MC), 1 ball Strawberry Passion #12 (A), 1 ball Yellow #11 (B)

● Size 4/E (3.50mm) aluminum crochet hook **or size needed to obtain gauge**

● Tapestry needle

● JHB International Buttons, ¾ in./1.9cm: 2 Sea Sheen #31231

Beach Shoes

● 1 ball Emerald #15 (MC), 1 ball Strawberry Passion #12 (A), 1 ball Yellow #11 (B)

The set

● 3 (4, 5, 6, 8) balls Emerald #15 (MC), 1 ball Strawberry Passion #12 (A), 1 ball Yellow #11 (B)

GAUGE

- In sc: 18 sts and 24 rows = 4 in./10.2 cm

- In dc: 18 sts and 15 rows = 4 in./10.2cm

SIZES

Dress

- For girls, 6 months (12 months, 18 months, 2 years, 4 years); directions are written for the smallest size with changes for the larger sizes in parentheses

Beach Shoes

- 3–6 (6–12) months

FINISHED MEASUREMENTS

Dress

- Chest: 15½ (18½, 22, 25, 28) in./ 39.4 (47, 55.9, 63.5, 71.1)cm

- Length: 13 (14½, 16, 17, 19) in./ 33 (36.9, 40.6, 43.3, 48.3)cm

Beach Shoes

- Sole length: 3½ (4) in./8.9 (10.2)cm

ABBREVIATIONS

- hdc2tog = in each of next 2 sts (yo and draw up lp), yo and draw through all 5 lps on hook

- sc2tog = draw up lp in each of next 2 sts, yo and draw through all 3 lps on hook

- sc3tog = draw up lp in each of next 3 sts, yo and draw through all 4 lps on hook

● ● ● ● ● ● ● ● ● ● ●

Before You Begin

- When making the Beach Shoes, note that the yellow sole will be slightly smaller than the green sole because of the dyes used to color the yarns.

  - Turn at the end of each row.

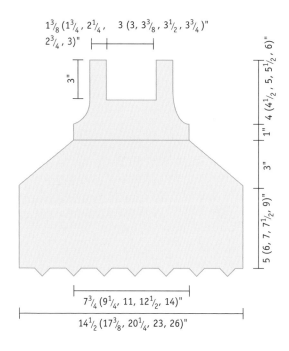

1³⁄₈ (1¾, 2¼,   3 (3, 3³⁄₈, 3½, 3¾)"
2¾, 3)"

3"

1" 4 (4½, 5, 5½, 6)"

1"

3"

5 (6, 7, 7½, 9)"

7¾ (9¼, 11, 12½, 14)"

14½ (17⅜, 20¼, 23, 26)"

• Dress •

BACK

Bodice

Beg at lower edge of bodice and with MC, ch 36 (43, 50, 57, 64).

Row 1 (RS): Sc in second ch from hook and in each ch across—35 (42, 49, 56, 63) sts.

Row 2: Ch 1, working in back lps, sc in each sc across.

Rep Row 2 until work measures 1 in./2.5cm from beg. Fasten off.

Armhole Shaping: Sk first 4 sts, join MC with sl st in back lp of next st. Working in back lps, sc in same sc as joining and in each of next 26 (32, 40, 47, 54) sts; turn, leaving last 4 sts unworked. Cont in back lp sc, dec 1 st each edge every other row 1 (2, 3, 4, 5) times—25 (29, 35, 40, 45) sts. Cont in pattern until piece measures approx 2 (2½, 3, 3½, 4) in./5.1 (6.4, 7.6, 8.9, 10.2)cm from beg, ending with WS row.

Left Shoulder: Work est pattern across first 6 (8, 10, 12, 14) sts. Cont in pattern until piece measures approx 5 (5½, 6, 6½, 7) in./12.7 (14, 15.2, 16.5, 17.8)cm from beg. Fasten off.

Right Shoulder: With RS facing, sk center 13 (13, 15, 16, 17) sts. Join MC with sl st in back lp of next st. Working in pattern, ch 1, sc in same lp as joining and in each of next 5 (7, 9, 11, 13) lps. Complete as for Left Shoulder.

Skirt

With RS facing and MC, work 35 (42, 49, 56, 63) sc evenly spaced along lower edge of bodice. Ch 1, sl st in back lp of each sc across.

Row 3: Ch 3 (counts as dc), dc in each rem lp across.

Row 4: Ch 1, sc in each dc across.

Row 5: Ch 3 (counts as dc), working in back lps of this and *each RS row hereafter,* dc in each of next 2 sc. (3 dc in next sc, dc in next 6 sc) across, ending 3 dc in next sc, dc in last 3 sc—45 (54, 63, 72, 81) sts.

Row 6: Ch 1, sc in each dc across.

Row 7: Ch 3 (counts as dc), dc in each sc across.

Row 8: Ch 1, sc in each dc across.

Row 9: Ch 3 (counts as dc), dc in each of next 3 sc. (3 dc in next sc, dc in next 8 sc) across, ending 3 dc in next sc, dc in last 4 sc—55 (66, 77, 88, 99) sts.

Rows 10–12: Rep Rows 6 to 8.

Row 13: Ch 3 (counts as dc), dc in each of next 4 sc; (3 dc in next sc, dc in next 10 sc) across, ending 3 dc in next sc, dc in last 5 sc—65 (78, 91, 104, 117) sts.

Rep Rows 6 to 7 for 6 (7, 9, 10, 12) times more. Rep Row 6 again. Skirt should measure approx 8 (9, 10, 10½, 12) in./20.3 (22.9, 25.4, 26.7, 30.5)cm from sl st row.

Last Row: Working in back lps, ch 1, sc in each of first 6 lps; (3 sc in next lp, sc in next 12 lps) across, ending 3 sc in next lp, sc in last 6 lps—75 (90, 105, 120, 135) sts. Fasten off.

FRONT

Work as for Back.

FINISHING

Join side seams.

Shell Edging

Holding RS of dress with bodice toward you, join A in ninth sl st from right seam on front. Ch 1, sc in same st as joining. Ch 11 for big lp, sk next 6 (4, 6, 6, 6) sts, sc in next st. * Ch 2, sk 3 sts, 9 dc in next st for Shell, ch 2, sk 2 sts, sc in next st; rep from * around, ending ch 2, sk 2 sts, Shell in next st, ch 2, sl st in first sc. Fasten off.

Rnd 2: Holding RS of dress with bodice toward you, join A with sl st in first sc to left of lp. Ch 1, sc in same sc as joining. * Sc in ch-2 sp, sc in 9 dc, sc in ch-2 sp, sc in next sc; rep from * around; turn.

Rnd 3: * Sl st in front lp of sc, sk 1 sc, sl st in front lp of next 9 sc, sk 1 sc; rep from * around, ending sl st in front lp of sc. Fasten off.

Rnd 4: With RS facing, join A with sl st in rem front lp of first sc to left of lp. * (Ch 1, sl st in each rem lp) around for rickrack trim. At end, fasten off. Take loose ends to WS and secure in place.

Big Fish

With B, ch 5. Sc in second ch from hook and in each ch across—4 sts.

Row 2: Ch 1, 2 sc in first sc, sc in 2 sc, 2 sc in last sc—6 sts.

Row 3: Ch 1, 2 sc in first sc, sc in 4 sc, 2 sc in last sc—8 sts.

Rows 4–7: Ch 1, sc in each sc across.

Row 8: Ch 1, sc2tog, sc in 4 sc, sc2tog—6 sts.

Row 9: Ch 1, sc2tog, sc in 2 sc, sc2tog—4 sts.

Row 10: Ch 1, (sc2tog) 2 times—2 sts.

Row 11 (RS): Fin: Ch 3 (counts as dc), 5 dc in first sc, in next sc [sl st, ch 3 (counts as dc), 5 dc]. Fasten off.

Completion: With RS facing, join B with sl st in last dc of Fin. Sl st over dc post, sl st evenly around fish, ending sl st over dc post, sl st in third ch of beg ch-3. Fasten off.

With RS facing, join A with sl st in fish head. Ch 9, sl st in fourth ch from right edge of big lp on shell edging. Sl st in each ch across, ending sl st in same sp as beg sl st. Fasten off. Weave loose ends on WS of fish.

Little Fish

With B, ch 4. Sc in second ch from hook and in each ch across—3 sts.

Row 2: Ch 1, 2 sc in first sc, sc in next sc, 2 sc in last sc—5 sts.

Rows 3–4: Ch 1, sc in each sc across.

Row 5: Ch 1, sc2tog, sc in next sc, sc2tog—3 sts.

Row 6: Ch 1, sc3tog—1 st.

Row 7 (RS): Fin: Ch 3 (counts as dc), 3 dc in sc, in same sc [sl st, ch 3 (counts as dc), 3 dc]. Fasten off.

Completion: Same as for Big Fish. Then join ch-9 in fourth ch from left edge of big lp on shell edging and work as for Big Fish. Lap little fish over big fish. Thread A into tapestry needle and make one st over the center st between the two fish on lp; secure in place on WS of dress.

Button Loops: Holding RS of dress *back* toward you, join MC with sl st in first sc on strap. Sl st in 2 (3, 4, 5, 6) sts, ch 2, sk 2 sts, sl st in 2 (3, 4, 5, 6) sts. Fasten off. Rep for second strap.

Try dress on child to determine button placement; then sew buttons onto center front of front straps.

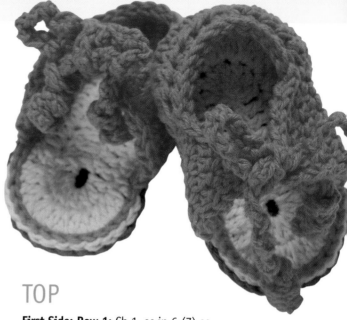

• Beach Shoes •

SOLES (make two)

First Sole: With MC ch 10 (12). 7 dc in fourth ch from hook, dc in each of next 5 (7) ch, 8 dc in last ch. Working along opposite side, dc in each of next 5 (7) ch; join with a sl st in third ch of beg ch-3. Ch 3 (counts as dc), 2 dc in each of next 7 dc, hdc in next 5 (7) dc, 2 dc in each of next 8 dc, hdc in next 5 (7) dc, dc in sp near beg ch-3. Join with sl st in third ch of beg ch-3. Fasten off.

Second Sole: With B, make another sole in the same manner.

Joining: Holding WSs tog, with A, draw lp through first hdc of each Sole. Sl st in each st around to join the soles—42 (46) sts. Do not fasten off.

SIDES AND HEEL

Row 1: Ch 1, sc into the first 6 (7) sl sts, hdc into next 14 (16) sl sts, sc into 6 (7) sl sts—26 (30) sts.

Row 2: Ch 1, sc in 6 (7) sc, hdc2tog, hdc in next 10 (12) hdc, hdc2tog, sc in 6 (7) sc—24 (26) sts.

Row 3: Rep Row 2.

Row 4: Ch 1, sc in rem 22 (26) sts.

A Different Look

For a quick accessory, make another little fish. Then with the same color yarn, chain 150; join with a slip stitch to form a circle. Next, (chain 1, slip stitch) in each chain around for the rickrack stitch; at the end, fasten off. Sew the little fish to the chain to make a necklace.

TOP

First Side: Row 1: Ch 1, sc in 6 (7) sc.

Row 2: Ch 1, sk 1 sc, sc in 3 (4) sc, sk 1 sc, sc in last sc.

Row 3: Ch 1, sc in 4 (5) sc.

Row 4: Ch 1, sk 1 sc, sc in 1 (2) sc, sk 1 sc, sc in last sc.

Row 5: Ch 1, sc in 2 (3) sc.

Row 6: Ch 1, sk 0 (1) sc, sc2tog. **For larger size only:** On the next row, ch 1, sc2tog.

Tie: Work 40 rows of ch 1, sc in sc; turn. Fasten off.

Second Side: With the outside facing, join A with a sl st in sixth (seventh) sc from edge. Work as for First Side.

With RS facing, draw up lp in edge near toe. Sl st to last row before working the single sc tie. Sl st along opposite edge, across heel; then on other side to match first side. Fasten off. Weave in loose ends.

FINISHING

Tie two to three overhand knots near the ends of the ties. Thread tail into a tapestry needle and back through the knots to hide it. Make a bow with the ties.

Waves

The graduating colors—like those of a lagoon—are put together with easy stitches to make this pullover a nice choice for any baby. The boat neck is modified by working one row of graduated stitches onto each shoulder. Make up the bunny as a quick gift that even an older child will love to cuddle.

Intermediate

MATERIALS

Sweater

- Stylecraft Satin Touch 100% acrylic (DK weight; distributed by S. R. Kertzer), 3.5-oz./100g skeins (each (248 yd./227m): 1 skein Bluebird #1394 (A), 1 skein Lilac Haze #1384 (B), 1 skein Hyacinth #1381 (C), 1 skein Clematis #1390 (D)

- Size 5/F (4.00mm) aluminum crochet hook **or size needed to obtain gauge**

- Tapestry needle

Bunny

- 1 skein Clematis #1390

- Scrap contrasting yarn for eyes

- Approx 1 yd./1m contrasting yarn for bow

- Size 4/E (3.5mm) aluminum crochet hook **or one size smaller than that needed to obtain gauge**

- Polyester fiberfill for stuffing

The Set

- 1 skein Lilac Haze #1384 (B), 1 skein Hyacinth #1381 (C), 1 skeins Clematis #1390 (D)

GAUGE

- In Body Pattern: 20 sts = 4 in./10.2cm; one 8-row pattern rep = 1½ in./3.8cm

- In sc: 18 sts and 20 rows = 4 in./10.2cm

SIZES

Sweater

- For wee ones, 6 (12, 18, 24) months; directions are written for the smallest size with changes for the larger sizes in parentheses

Bunny

- One size

FINISHED MEASUREMENTS

Sweater

- Chest: 20½ (22, 25, 27) in./52.1 (55.9, 63.5, 68.6)cm

- Length: 9½ (11, 12½, 14) in./24.2 (27.9, 31.8, 35.6)cm

Bunny

- Height: 6 in./15.2cm to top of head

ABBREVIATIONS

- sc2tog = draw up lp in each of next 2 sts, yo and draw through all 3 lps on hook

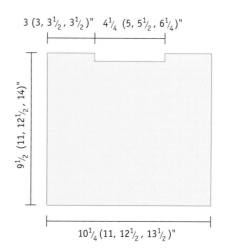

3 (3, 3½, 3½)"   4¼ (5, 5½, 6¼)"

9½ (11, 12½, 14)"

10¼ (11, 12½, 13½)"

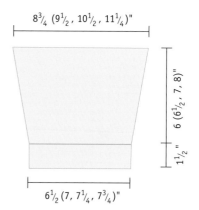

8¾ (9½, 10½, 11¼)"

6 (6½, 7, 8)"

1½"

6½ (7, 7¼, 7¾)"

● ● ● ● ● ● ● ● ● ● ●

Before You Begin

- Note that the cuff is added after the arm of sleeve has been completed.

- Turn at the end of each row.

PATTERN STITCHES

Body Pattern

multiple of 4 sts + 3 sts; rep of 8 rows

Row 1 (WS): Ch 1, sl st in back lp of each st across; turn.

Row 2: Ch 1, sc in each rem lp across; turn.

Rows 3–4: Rep Rows 1 and 2.

Row 5: Rep Row 1.

Row 6: Ch 1, working in rem lps, sc in first 3 lps; * ch 1, sk 1 lp, sc in next 3 lps; rep from * across; turn.

Row 7: Ch 3 (counts as dc); dc in each sc and ch-1 sp across; turn.

Row 8: Ch 1, sc in first dc; tr in sk lp from Row 6, sk dc behind the tr. * Sc in each of next 3 dc, tr in same sk lp as before until 2 lps rem on hook, tr in next sk lp until 3 lps rem on hook, yo and draw through all 3 lps on hook, sk dc behind trs; rep from * across. At end, tr in same lp as last tr, sk 1 dc, sc in third ch of turning ch; turn.

Rep Rows 1 to 8 for Body Pattern.

• Sweater •

BACK

Beg at lower edge with A, ch 52 (56, 64, 68). Sc in second ch from hook and in each ch across—51 (55, 63, 67) sts. Rep Body Pattern Rows 1 to 8 twice; then rep Rows 1 to 7. Change to B and work Body Pattern Row 8. Rep Body Pattern Rows 1 to 8 once; then rep Rows 1 to 7. Change to C and work Body Pattern Row 8. Rep Body Pattern Rows 1 to 8 for 1 (2, 3, 4) times. With C, rep Body Pattern Rows 1 to 5.

Shoulders: Ch 1, working in rem lps, sc in first 5 (5, 6, 6) lps, hdc in next 5 (5, 6, 6) lps, dc in next 5 (5, 6, 6) lps. Fasten off. Sk 21 (25, 27, 31) lps for neck. Join C with sl st in next lp. Ch 3 (counts as dc), dc in next 4 (4, 5, 5) lps, hdc in next 5 (5, 6, 6) lps, sc in last 5 (5, 6, 6) lps. Fasten off.

FRONT

Work as for Back.

SLEEVES (make two)

With D, ch 30 (32, 34, 36). Sc in second ch from hook and in each ch across—29 (31, 33, 35) sts. Ch 1, sc in each sc across; turn. Cont in sc, inc 1 st each edge every fourth row 5 (6, 7, 8) times. Work even on the 39 (43, 47, 51) sts to approx 5 (5½, 6, 7) in./12.7 (14, 15.2, 17.8)cm from beg, ending with WS row.

Next RS row: Ch 1, sc in 3 sc, (ch 1, sk 1 sc, sc in next 3 sc) across.

Next Row (WS): Ch 3 (counts as dc), dc in each sc across.

Rep Body Pattern Row 8. Ch 1, sc in each st across and fasten off.

Cuff

With WS facing, join D with sl st in first rem ch of beg foundation. Ch 1, work 29 (31, 33, 35) sc across; sl st in front lp of first sc.

Rnd 2: Sl st in front lp of each sc around.

Rnd 3: Sc in each rem lp around.

Rnds 4–9: Rep Rnds 2 to 3.

Rnd 10: Rep Rnd 2. Fasten off.

FINISHING

Join shoulder seams.

Place markers 4¾ (5, 5½, 6) in./12 (12.7, 14, 15.2)cm from shoulder seam on front and back. Set in sleeves between markers. Join underarm and side seams. Turn back cuffs.

• Bunny •

HEAD AND BODY

Beg at the top of head, with D, ch 2.

Rnd 1: 6 sc in second ch from hook.

Rnd 2: 2 sc in each sc around—12 sts.

Rnd 3: (Sc in next sc, 2 sc in next sc) around—18 sts.

Rnd 4: (Sc in next 2 sc, 2 sc in next sc) around—24 sts.

Rnds 5–8: Sc in each sc around.

Rnd 9 (Neck): Sc2tog around—12 sts.

Rnd 10: Sc in each sc around.

Rnd 11: 2 sc in each sc around—24 sts.

Rnd 12 (Shoulders): (Sc in 10 sc, 2 sc in each of next 2 sc) twice—28 sts.

Rnds 13–20: Sc in each sc around.

LEGS

First Leg: Row 1: In back lps, sc in 14 sc; turn.

Row 2: Ch 1, sc in 12 sc, sc2tog; turn.

Row 3: Ch 1, sc in 11 sc, sc2tog; turn.

Row 4: Ch 1, sc in 10 sc, sc2tog; turn.

Row 5: Ch 1, sc in 9 sc, sc2tog; turn.

Row 6 (Foot): Ch 1, (sc2tog) 5 times; turn.

Rnd 7: 2 sc in first sc of Row 6, 2 sc in each of next 4 sc—10 sts.

Rnds 8–9: Sc in each sc around.

Rnd 10: Sc2tog around—5 sts. Leaving a tail, fasten off. Take tail to inside of foot.

Second Leg: Work as for First Leg.

Stuffing: Firmly stuff head and body—do not stuff legs. Join leg and crotch seams.

ARMS (make two)

Join yarn with sl st in shoulder area. Ch 1, sc down side for 4 sts; then turn and work 4 sc behind first sts. Sc in each sc around for 3 more rnds. Sc2tog around—4 sts. 2 sc in each sc around—8 sts. Sc in each of 8 sc around. Sc2tog around. Cut yarn, leaving 6-in./15.2cm tail.

Thread tail into tapestry needle and back through front lps of rem 4 sts. Pull up to close opening. Take tail to inside of arm.

FACE

Thread a long double strand of D into needle. Locate center of face. Leaving 3-in./7.6cm tail at beg and end and working over two rows, sew over and over until bump looks like a nose. Make st in center over yarn tails and just beneath nose. Trim tails and fray to look like whiskers. Thread contrasting yarn into needle, make 1 slanted st on either side of nose for eyes.

A Different Look

The bunny is made from yarn left over after crocheting the sweater. Why not make the bunny's head, body, and appendages in different colors? Or get really creative and make the bunny in stripes to match the sweater.

EARS (make two)

At top of head, make 6 sc around. Sc in each sc around 3 more times. Sc2tog, sc in 4 sc. Sc2tog, sc in 3 sc. Leaving a tail, fasten off. Thread tail into needle and back through front lps of rem 4 sts; pull up to close opening. Hide tail on inside of ear.

BOW

With contrasting yarn, ch 100 and fasten off. Weave ch through openings at neck. Tie into a bow; then tie the bow into a bow.

Sailor Jacket

● ●

Purchased trims in gold and bright anchor buttons are added to this jacket to ensure that your little skipper will travel first class. Toeless booties and a sailor hat complete the ensemble.

MATERIALS

Jacket

- J. & P. Coats' Luster Sheen 100% acrylic (machine-washable, sport weight), 1.8-oz./51g balls (each 150 yd./137m): 5 (6, 7, 8) balls of Rally Red #910

- Size 3/D (3.25mm) aluminum crochet hook **or size needed to obtain gauge**

- Tapestry needle

- JHB International Buttons, ⅝ in./ 1.6cm in diameter: 3 Ship's Ahoy #97158 (Gold/Navy)

- Wrights Middy Braid, ³⁄₁₆ in./ 4.8mm wide, 1 package Metallic #PC10

- Hirschberg Schutz Iron-On embellishment: 1 Anchor in antique gold #AP4773-05

- Sewing needle

- Gold thread

Booties

- 1 ball Rally Red #910

Hat

- 2 balls Rally Red #910

- 1 package Middy Braid: Metallic #PC10

- 1 button, Ship's Ahoy

The Set

- 7 (8, 9, 10) balls Rally Red #910
- 1 package Middy Braid: Metallic #PC10
- 4 buttons, Ship's Ahoy

GAUGE

- In Body Pattern: 26 sts = 5 in./12.7cm; 33 rows = 6 in./15.2 cm

SIZES

Jacket

- For wee ones, 6 (12, 18, 24) months; directions are written for the smallest size with changes for the larger sizes in parentheses

Booties

- One size: 3–6 months

Hat

- One size

FINISHED MEASUREMENTS

Jacket

- Chest (buttoned): 20½ (22¾, 25, 29) in./ 52.1 (57.8, 63.5, 73.7)cm
- Length: 11 (12½, 13½, 15) in./27.9 (31.8, 34.3, 38.1)cm

Booties

- Sole length: 3½ in./8.9cm

Hat

- Circumference: 19 in./48.3cm

ABBREVIATIONS

- sc2tog = draw up lp in each of next 2 sts, yo and draw through all 3 lps on hook
- fpdc = front post double crochet: yo, insert hook from front to back then to front to go around dc post, draw up lp, (yo and draw through 2 lps on hook) twice
- fpdc over fpdc = on RS, fpdc over fpdc 2 rows below, skipping sc behind new st; on WS, sc in top of fpdc

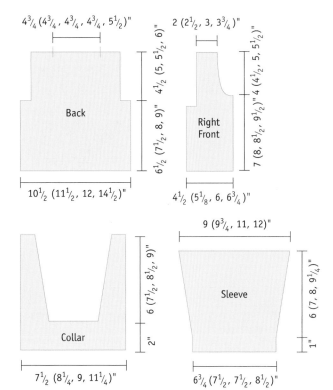

● ● ● ● ● ● ● ● ● ● ○ ○

Before You Begin

- Note that the cuff is added after the arm of the sleeve has been completed.
- Although the anchor can be ironed on, I recommend that you use gold sewing thread and a needle to attach it to the pocket.
- The hat is an intermediate project but is still easy. Rather than joining rounds, make the first stitch of next round into the first stitch of the last round.
- Turn at the end of each row.

PATTERN STITCH

Body Pattern

Row 1 (RS): Ch 1, sc in first sc; * ch 1, sk 1 sc, sc in each of next 3 sc; rep from * across, ending ch 1, sk 1 sc, sc in last sc.

Row 2: Ch 1, sc in each sc and ch-1 sp across.

Row 3: Ch 1, sc in first sc; * dc in skipped sc two rows below, sc in next sc, ch 1, sk 1 sc, sc in next sc; rep from * across, ending dc in skipped sc two rows below, sc in last sc.

Row 4: Ch 1, sc in each sc, dc, and ch-1 sp across.

Row 5: Ch 1, sc in first sc; * ch 1, sk 1 sc, sc in next sc, dc in sk sc two rows below, sc in next sc; rep from * across ending ch 1, sk 1 sc, sc in last sc.

Row 6: Rep Row 4.

Rep Rows 3 to 6 for Body Pattern.

• Jacket •

BACK

Beg at lower edge, ch 56 (60, 64, 76).

Foundation: Sc in second ch from hook and in each ch across—55 (59, 63, 75) sts.

Body Pattern: Work Rows 1 to 6 of Body Pattern. Rep Rows 3 to 6 to approx 6½ (7½, 8, 9) in./16.5 (19.1, 20.3, 22.9)cm from beg, ending ready to work Row 3.

Armhole Shaping: Sl st in first sc, hdc in ch-1 sp two rows below, sl st in each of next 2 sts. Work est pattern across to last 4 sts; sl st in each of next 2 sts, hdc in ch-1 sp two rows below, sl st in last sc and fasten off.

With WS facing, join yarn in fifth st from edge. Ch 1, sc in same sc as joining; work est pattern across next 46 (50, 54, 66) sts. Cont Body Pattern on rem 47 (51, 55, 67) sts to approx 11 (12½, 13½, 15) in./27.9 (31.8, 34.3, 39.4)cm from beg, ending with WS row.

Last Row: Ch 1, sc in first sc; sc in each sc across, working a hdc in each ch-1 sp two rows below.

RIGHT FRONT

Beg at lower edge, ch 24 (28, 32, 36). Work Foundation as for Back—23 (27, 31, 35) sts. Work Body Pattern as

for Back to approx 6½ (7½, 8, 9) in./16.5 (19.1, 20.3, 22.9)cm from beg, ending ready to work Row 3.

Armhole Shaping: Work est pattern across to last 4 sts; sl st in each of next 2 sts, hdc in ch-1 sp two rows below, sl st in last sc and fasten off.

With WS facing, join yarn in fifth st from edge. Ch 1, sc in same sc as joining; work est pattern to end. Cont in pattern on rem 19 (23, 27, 31) sts to approx 7 (8, 8½, 9½) in./17.8 (20.3, 21.6, 24.2)cm from beg, ending ready to work Row 3.

Neck Shaping: Sl st in first sc, hdc in ch-1 sp two rows below; cont pattern across; turn. Work est pattern across, leaving hdc and sl st unworked. Rep last two rows 3 (4, 5, 5) times more. Cont in pattern on rem 11 (13, 15, 19) sts until piece measures approx 11 (12½, 13½, 15) in./27.9 (31.8, 34.3, 39.4)cm from beg, ending with WS row. Rep Last Row as for Back.

LEFT FRONT

Work as for Right Front to approx 6½ (7½, 8, 9) in./ 16.5 (19.1, 20.3, 22.9)cm from beg, ending ready to work Row 5.

Armhole Shaping: Sl st in first sc, hdc in ch-1 sp two rows below, sl st in each of next 2 sts; work est pattern to end. Cont pattern on rem 19 (23, 27, 31) sts to approx 7 (8, 8½, 9½) in./17.8 (20.3, 21.6, 24.2)cm from beg, ending ready to work Row 3.

Neck Shaping: Work est pattern across to last 2 sts, hdc in ch-1 sp two rows below, sk last sc. Ch 1, sk hdc, work est pattern across. Rep last two rows 3 (4, 5, 5) times more. Cont in pattern on rem 11 (13, 15, 19) sts to approx 11 (12½, 13½, 15) in./27.9 (31.8, 34.3, 39.4)cm from beg, ending with WS row. Rep Last Row as for Back.

SLEEVES (make two)

Beg at lower edge, ch 36 (40, 40, 44). Rep Foundation as for Back—35 (39, 39, 43) sts. Work Body Pattern Rows 1 to 2. Including new sts into Body Pattern as they accumulate, beg with Row 3, inc 1 st each edge every fourth row 6 (6, 9, 10) times. Work even on 47 (51, 57, 63) sts to 6 (7, 8, 9¼) in./15.2 (17.8, 20.3, 23.5)cm from beg, ending with WS row. Rep Last Row as for Back.

COLLAR

Beg at lower edge, ch 40 (44, 48, 60). Rep Foundation as for Back—39 (43, 47, 59) sts. Work Body Pattern Rows 1 to 6; rep Rows 3 to 6 until piece measures approx 2 in./5.1 cm from beg, ending ready to work Row 3.

A Different Look

If you'd like, make this outfit in blue to match your baby's eyes.

First Side: Work Row 3 across first 9 (11, 13, 17) sts. Cont in pattern for two rows. Keeping to est pattern, dec 1 st at neck edge every other row 0 (0, 2, 8) times, then every fourth row 6 (8, 8, 6) times. Work even on rem 3 sts to 8 (9½, 10½, 11)/20.3 (24.2, 26.7, 27.9)cm from beg, ending with RS row. Fasten off.

Second Side: With WS facing, sk center 21 (21, 21, 25) sts. Join yarn with a sl st in next st. Ch 1, work Row 3 across last 9 (11, 13, 17) sts. Cont as for First Side.

Edging

With RS facing, join yarn with sl st at left edge of lower collar. Ch 1, work 42 (50, 55, 58) sc evenly spaced along outside edge; 2 sc in corner, 37 (41, 45, 57) sc across back, 2 sc in corner, 42 (50, 55, 58) sc to lower edge.

Row 2: Working in front lps, ch 1, sc in 42 (50, 55, 58) sc, 2 sc in corner, sc in 39 (43, 47, 59) sc, 2 sc in corner, sc in 42 (50, 55, 58) sc.

Row 3: Working through both lps, sc in 43 (51, 56, 59) sc, 2 sc in corner, sc in 39 (43, 47, 59) sc, 2 sc in corner, sc in 43 (51, 56, 59) sc.

Row 4: Ch 1, sc in 43 (51, 56, 59) sc, 2 sc in corner, sc in 41 (45, 49, 61) sc, 2 sc in corner, sc in 43 (51, 56, 59) sc.

Row 5: Sl st in each sc around and fasten off.

POCKET

Beg at lower edge, ch 16. Rep Foundation as for Back— 15 sts. Work Body Pattern Rows 1 to 6; rep Rows 3 to 6 twice. Rep Last Row as for Back. Work two sc rows on 15 sts. With RS facing, ch 1, sl st evenly along side of pocket, across lower edge, and along second side. For top of pocket, sl st in first sc, (ch 1, sl st in next sc) across for rickrack trim. At end, sl st in beg sl st and fasten off.

FINISHING

Join shoulder seams. Set in sleeves. Join underarm and side seams.

Pocket: Center anchor onto pocket and sew in place. Place pocket onto left front about ½ in./1.3cm from collar edge and 1¼ in./3.2cm from edge of front band. Pin in place so that pocket is straight. Use tapestry needle and yarn to join in place, leaving the top open.

Lower Sleeve: With RS facing, join yarn with sl st in seam. Ch 1, work 35 (39, 39, 43) sc evenly around. Sc in back lp of each sc around. Working in both lps, work 4 more sc rnds. Join with sl st in first sc of last rnd and fasten off.

Sew braid to front lps, beg at the seam. At end, leave about ½ in./1.3cm free; turn under and hold over the first raw edge. Sew around the fold; then sew rem edge of the braid.

Right Front Band: With RS facing, join yarn with sl st in lower right edge. Ch 1, work 40 (46, 48, 54) sc evenly spaced along edge to first V-neck shaping row; turn. Work 4 more sc rows. Fasten off.

Left Front Band: With RS facing, join yarn with a sl st in first V-neck shaping row. Work 40 (46, 48, 54) sc evenly spaced to lower edge. Ch 1, sc in each sc across. Ch 1, sc in sc; [ch 3, sk 3 sc, sc in each of next 8 (9, 10, 11) sc] 2 times, ch 3, sk 3 sc, sc in each rem sc to end. Sc in each sc across working 3 sc in each ch-3 sp. Work one more sc row. Fasten off.

With RS facing, join yarn with sl st in first sc at left neck edge. **For rickrack trim:** (ch 1, sl st in next sc) to corner, cont in (ch 1, sl st) across band, lower edge, next band, and then along right front. Fasten off. Sew buttons opposite buttonholes.

Collar: Holding RS of collar against WS of jacket, sl st in place. Sew band tops to collar edges. With needle and sewing thread, leaving 1 in./2.5cm at each end, sew

braid to collar along the lps rem from Row 2 of Collar Edging. Turn braid to inside of collar, fold under, and sew around all three edges. Sew outside edge of braid to collar; then turn loose end to WS of collar and complete as before.

• Booties •

SOLE

Ch 12. 7 dc in fourth ch from hook, dc in next 7 ch, 8 dc in last ch. Working along opposite edge, dc in 7 dc; join with sl st in third ch of beg ch-3. Ch 3 (counts as dc), 2 dc in each of next 7 dc, hdc in 7 dc, 2 dc in next 8 dc, hdc in 7 dc, dc in sp before first dc; join and fasten off.

TOP

With RS facing, join with sl st in first hdc.

Row 1: Ch 1, 2 sc in first hdc, sc in next 6 hdc, sc2tog, sc in 12 dc, sc2tog, sc in 6 hdc, 2 sc in last hdc.

Row 2: Ch 1, sc in 8 sc, hdc in 14 sc, sc in 8 sc.

Row 3: Ch 1, 2 sc in first sc, sc in 7 sc, sc2tog, sc in 10 hdc, sc2tog, sc in 7 sc, 2 sc in last sc.

Row 4: Ch 1, sc in 9 sc, hdc in 12 sc, sc in 9 sc.

Row 5: Ch 1, 2 sc in first sc, sc in each st around, working 2 sc in last sc—32 sts.

Row 6: Ch 1, sc in each sc around.

Row 7: Rep Row 5—34 sts.

Rep Rows 6 to 7 twice more—38 sts.

First bootie: Lap right over left side, leaving 4 rows free on each side. Working through both layers and around the toe opening, sc in 8 sc, 4 sc along side, 16 sc along toe, 4 sc in side. Sl st in back lp of each sc around. Sl st in front lp of each sc around and fasten off.

Second bootie: Lap left side over right side and complete as before.

• Hat •

CAP

Beg at crown, ch 2.

Rnd 1: 6 sc in second ch from hook.

Rnd 2: In each sc (sc, dc) around—12 sts.

Rnd 3: (2 sc in sc, dc in dc) around—18 sts.

Rnd 4: (2 sc in each of 2 sc, fpdc in dc two rnds below) around—30 sts.

Rnd 5: (2 sc in first sc, sc in next 2 sc, 2 sc in next sc, fpdc over fpdc) around—42 sts.

Rnd 6: (2 sc in first sc, sc in next 4 sc, 2 sc in next sc, fpdc over fpdc) around—54 sts.

Rnds 7–12: (2 sc in first sc, sc in each sc around, working 2 sc in last sc, fpdc over fpdc) around. After Rnd 12—126 sts.

Rnd 13: (2 sc in each of 20 sc, fpdc over fpdc) around—246 sts.

Rnds 14–16: (Sc in 40 sc, fpdc over fpdc) around.

Rnd 17: * Sc in first 4 sc, (sc2tog, sc in 3 sc) 7 times, sc in last sc, fpdc over fpdc; rep from * around—204 sts.

Rnd 18: * Sc in first 2 sc, (sc2tog, sc in 2 sc) 7 times, sc2tog, sc in next sc, fpdc over fpdc; rep from * around—156 sts.

Rnd 19: (Sc in 25 sc, fpdc over fpdc) around.

Rnd 20: * Sc in 1 sc, (sc2tog, sc in 3 sc) 4 times, sc2tog, sc in 2 sc, fpdc over fpdc; rep from * around—126 sts.

Rnd 21: (Sc in 20 sc, fpdc over fpdc) around.

Rnd 22: * Sc in 1 sc, (sc2tog, sc in 2 sc) 4 times, sc2tog, sc in 1 sc, fpdc over fpdc; rep from * around—96 sts.

Rnds 23–26: (Sc in 15 sc, fpdc over fpdc) around. After Rnd 26, *turn.*

BAND

Row 1: Ch 1, sc in each st across; turn.

Rows 2–8: Rep Row 1.

Tab: Ch 1, work 9 sc across band edge. Ch 1, sc2tog, sc in 5 sc, sc2tog; turn. Work 3 rows of sc on the 7 sts. Ch 1, sc in 2 sc, ch 3, sk 3 sc, sc in 2 sc. Ch 1, working 3 sc in ch-3 sp, sc in each sc across. Ch 1, sc2tog, sc in 3 sc, sc2tog. Ch 1, sc2tog, sc in 1 sc, sc2tog. Ch 1, draw up lp in each of 3 sc, yo and draw through all 4 lps on hook. Fasten off.

With the RS facing, work rickrack trim as for Front finishing, beg at corner of button side of band. Work around entire band and around tab. Fold band to inside of cap and cont in rickrack trim, working between the sts on Band Row 1. When you reach the opposite side, fasten off. Hide ends.

Sew button opposite buttonhole.

Quackers

● ●

Beginner

Three ducklings are sewn onto this pullover with clever waves brushing their little wings. Note the buttoned shoulders for easy over-the-head dressing. With the webbed duck boots and the sun hat, your little one will be ready for anything.

MATERIALS

Sweater

- Patons' Look at Me! 60% acrylic/40% nylon (sport weight; distributed by Spinrite Inc.), 1.75-oz./50g balls (each 152 yd./139m): 2 (2, 3, 3) balls White #6351 (MC), 1 ball Cornflower Blue #6365 (A), 1 yd./1m Orange #6385 (B)

- Patons' Astra 100% acrylic (sport weight; distributed by Spinrite Inc.), 1.75-oz./50g balls (each 178 yd./162.6m): 1 ball School Bus Yellow #2941 (C)

- Size 4/E (3.50mm) aluminum crochet hook **or size needed to obtain gauge**

- Size 3/D (3.25mm) aluminum crochet hook

- Tapestry needle

- JHB International Buttons, ⅝ in./ 1.6cm in diameter: 6 America III #98034 (Blue/Red/Gold)

Sun Hat
- Look at Me!: 1 ball White #6351

Duck Boots
- Astra: 1 ball School Bus Yellow #2941

The Set

- Look at Me!: 3 (3, 4, 4) balls White #6351, 1 ball Cornflower Blue #6365, 1 yd./1m Orange #6385

- Astra: 1 ball School Bus Yellow #2941

GAUGE

- In Body Pattern with larger hook: 17 sts and 12 rows = 4 in./10.2cm

SIZES

Sweater

- For wee ones, 6 (12, 18, 24) months; directions are written for the smallest size with changes for the larger sizes in parentheses

Sun Hat

- One size

Duck Boots

- One size

FINISHED MEASUREMENTS

Sweater

- Chest: 20 (22, 25, 27) in. /50.8 (55.9, 63.5, 68.6)cm

- Length: 9½ (11, 12½, 14) in./24.2 (27.9, 31.8, 36.9)cm

Sun Hat

- Circumference: 17 in./43.2cm

Duck Boots

- Length: approx 3½ in./8.9cm

ABBREVIATIONS

- sc2tog = draw up lp in each of next 2 sts, yo and draw through all 3 lps on hook

● ● ● ● ● ● ● ● ● ○ ○ ○

Before You Begin

- Note that the ducks are placed between the waves and the sweater; the waves are then tacked to the sweater and, where appropriate, to the ducks.

- Turn at the end of each row.

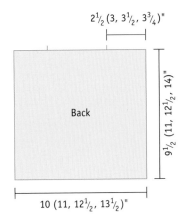

2½ (3, 3½, 3¾)"

Back

9½ (11, 12½, 14)"

10 (11, 12½, 13½)"

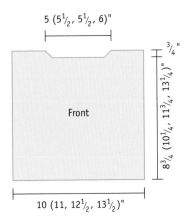

5 (5½, 5½, 6)"

Front

¾"

8¾ (10¼, 11¾, 13¼)"

10 (11, 12½, 13½)"

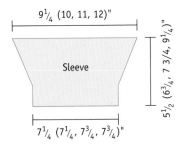

9¼ (10, 11, 12)"

Sleeve

5½ (6¾, 7 3/4, 9¼)"

7¼ (7¼, 7¾, 7¾)"

PATTERN STITCH

Body Pattern

any multiple; rep of 2 rows

Row 1 (RS): Ch 3 (counts as dc); dc in each sc across; turn.

Row 2: Ch 1, sc in each dc across; turn.

Rep Rows 1 to 2 for Body Pattern.

• Sweater •

BACK

Beg at lower edge with larger hook and A, ch 45 (49, 55, 59).

Foundation: Row 1: Dc in fourth ch from hook and in each ch across—43 (47, 53, 57) sts; turn.

Row 2: Ch 1, sc in each dc across; turn.

Beg Body Pattern, rep Rows 1 to 2 for 2 (3, 4, 5) times.

Waves: Working in front lps for this row only, sl in first 1 (1, 2, 2) sc; * in next st (sc, hdc, 3 dc, hdc, sc) **, sl st in each of next 3 sc; rep from * across, ending last rep at **, sl st in last 1 (1, 2, 2) sc. Fasten off.

Body: With WS facing and larger hook, join MC with sl st

in first rem lp. Ch 1, sc in same lp as joining and in each rem lp across—43 (47, 53, 57) sts.

Cont in Body Pattern to approx 9½ (11, 12½, 14) in./ 24.2 (27.9, 31.8, 35.6)cm from beg, ending with WS row. Fasten off.

FRONT

Work as for Back to approx 8¾ (10¼, 11¾, 13¼) in./ 22.2 (26, 29.8, 33.6)cm from beg, ending with WS row.

Neck Shaping: Left Shoulder: Ch 3 (counts as dc), dc in each of next 8 (9, 12, 13) sc, dc2tog, dc in next sc; turn. Ch 1, sc in each of 11 (12, 15, 16) rem sts. Fasten off.

Right Shoulder: Sk center 19 (21, 21, 23) sts. With the RS facing join MC with sl st in next st. Ch 3 (counts as dc), dc2tog, dc in each rem sc to end; turn. Ch 1, sc in each of 11 (12, 15, 16) rem sts. Fasten off.

SLEEVES (make two)

Beg at lower edge with larger hook and A, ch 33 (33, 35, 35). Work Foundation Rows 1 to 2 as for Back—31 (31, 33, 33) sts.

Rep Body Pattern, Rows 1 to 2 for 1 (2, 3, 3) times more.

Rep Waves as for Back.

Change to MC and sc in each rem lp across—31 (31, 33, 33) sts. Cont with MC for remainder of sleeve, inc 1 st each edge every other row 3 (6, 7, 9) times and then every fourth row 1 (0, 0, 0) times—39 (43, 47, 51) sts. Work even to approx 5½ (6¾, 7¾, 9¼) in./14 (17.1, 19.7, 23.5)cm from beg, ending with WS row. Fasten off.

DUCKS (make three)

Beg at head, with smaller hook and C, ch 3.

Row 1: Sc in second ch from hook and next ch; turn.

Row 2: Ch 1, 2 sc in each of two sc; turn.

Row 3: Ch 1, 2 sc in first sc, sc in next two sc, 2 sc in last sc—6 sts; turn.

Row 4: Ch 1, sc in each of first 5 sc, leaving last st unworked; turn.

Row 5: Sl st in first sc, sc in rem 4 sc; turn.

Row 6: Ch 1, 3 sc in first sc, 2 sc in second sc; leave rem sts unworked; turn.

Row 7: Ch 1, 2 sc in first sc, sc in 4 sc—6 sts; turn.

Row 8: Ch 1, sc in first 5 sc, 2 sc in last sc—7 sts; turn.

Row 9: Ch 1, 2 sc in first sc, sc in each sc across—8 sts; turn.

Row 10: Ch 1, sc2tog, sc in each of next 5 sc, 3 sc in last sc—9 sts; turn.

Row 11: Ch 1, 2 sc in first sc, sc in each sc across, working sc2tog over last 2 sts—9 sts; turn.

With RS facing and working toward tail, (ch 1, sl st) in each st and row around entire duck, for rickrack edging. Fasten off.

FINISHING

Attach Ducks: Position first duck with the left side of head at center front. Place second duck approx 2 in./ 10.2cm from first. Make sure ducks are under waves; sew in place. Tack waves to front and onto ducks where appropriate. Place third duck onto back approx 1½ in./ 3.8cm from right side edge; attach as before and tack waves as before.

Thread a double strand of A in tapestry needle and make one tiny straight stitch eye on each duck; then work over same st again. Thread a double strand of C in needle and make two long straight sts for bill on each duck; then work over same sts again.

Front Neck: With RS facing and larger hook, join MC with sl st in side of first st at right neck edge. Ch 1, work 25 (27, 27, 29) sc evenly spaced along neck, leaving shoulder sts free; turn. **Rows 2–3:** Ch 1, sc in each sc across; turn. After Row 3, fasten off.

Back Right Shoulder: With RS facing and larger hook, join MC with sl st in first st at right shoulder edge. Ch 1, sc in same st as joining and in each of next 10 (11, 14, 15) sts; turn. Ch 1, sc in each sc across; turn. Ch 1, sc in first 3 (4, 5, 4) sc, [ch 1, sk 1 sc, sc in next 3 (3, 4, 5) sc] twice; turn. Ch 1, sc in each sc and ch-1 sp across. Fasten off.

Left Back Shoulder: With RS facing and larger hook, join MC with sl st in first st at left shoulder edge. Work 2 sc rows on 11 (12, 15, 16) sts. Ch 1, [sc in 3 (3, 4, 5) sc, ch 1, sk 1 sc] twice, sc in last 3 (4, 5, 4) sts; turn. Ch 1, sc in each sc and ch-1 sp across. Fasten off.

Back Neck: With RS facing and larger hook, join MC with sl st in side of first st at right neck edge. Ch 1, work 30 (32, 32, 34) sc evenly spaced along neck, leaving shoulder sts free; turn. Work two more sc rows; fasten off.

Sewing: Sew buttons opposite buttonholes with two on the last sc row of front shoulders and one at each neck edge.

With sweater buttoned, join shoulder edges.

Place markers 4¾ (5, 5½, 6) in./12 (12.7, 14, 15.2)cm each side of shoulder seams. Set in sleeves between markers. Using matching yarn, join underarm and side seams.

Edgings: Sleeves: To slightly pull in cuff, sl st around lower edge and evenly sk 6 (5, 4, 3) sts. **Lower edge of sweater:** Work (ch 1, sl st) for rickrack trim in each rem Foundation ch; at end, join and fasten off.

• Sun Hat •
CAP

Beg at crown, with larger hook, ch 4; work 11 dc in fourth ch from hook—12 sts; join with sl st in third ch of beg ch-4.

Rnd 2: Ch 1, 2 sc in same st as joining; 2 sc in each dc around—24 sts; join.

Rnd 3: Ch 3 (counts as dc); dc in each sc around; join.

Rnd 4: Rep Rnd 2—48 sts.

Rnd 5: Rep Rnd 3.

Rnd 6: Ch 1, (sc in sc, 2 sc in next sc) around—72 sts; join.

Rnd 7: Rep Rnd 3.

Rnd 8: Ch 1, sc in same st as joining and in each dc around; join.

Rnd 9: Rep Rnd 3.

Rnd 10: Ch 3 (counts as dc); dc in each dc around; join.

Rnds 11–12: Rep Rnds 2 to 3.

BRIM

Rnd 13: Ch 1, sc in back lp of each st around; join.

Rnd 14 and all even numbered rnds: Rep Rnd 13.

Rnd 15: Ch 1, in back lps (sc in each of 5 sc, 2 sc in next sc) around—84 sts; join.

Rnd 17: Ch 1, in back lps (sc in each of 6 sc, 2 sc in next sc) around—96 sts; join.

Rnd 19: Ch 1, in back lps (sc in each of 7 sc, 2 sc in next sc) around—108 sts; join.

Rnd 21: (Ch 1, sl st in next sc) around for rickrack edging. At end, join and fasten off.

TIE

With larger hook and a double strand of yarn, ch 150. Sl st in second ch from hook and in each ch across. Fasten off. Weave through Rnd 12. Try Sun Hat on baby before tying ends of tie into a square knot. Knot ends.

• Duck Boots •
SOLE

With smaller hook, ch 11.

Rnd 1 (RS): 7 dc in fourth ch from hook, hdc in next 2 ch, sc in next 2 ch, hdc in next 2 ch, 8 dc in last ch. Working along opposite edge of foundation, hdc in 2 ch, sc in 2 ch, hdc in 2 ch. Join with sl st in third ch of beg ch-3.

Rnd 2: Ch 3 (counts as dc), dc in same st as joining. Work 2 dc in each of next 7 dc, hdc in 2 hdc, sc in 2 sc,

hdc in 2 hdc, 2 dc in each of next 8 dc, hdc in 2 hdc, sc in 2 sc, hdc in 2 hdc—44 sts; join. Fasten off.

TOP

With smaller hook, ch 6. Sc in second ch from hook and in next 3 ch, 5 sc in last ch. Working along opposite edge of foundation, sc in 4 ch—13 sts; turn.

Row 2: Ch 1, sc in first 4 sc, 2 sc in each of next 5 sc, sc in last 4 sc—18 sts; turn.

Row 3: Ch 1, sc in first 4 sc, 2 sc in next sc; (sc in next sc, 2 sc in next sc) 4 times, sc in 5 sc—23 sts; turn.

Row 4: Ch 1, sc in first 4 sc, 2 sc in next sc; (sc in next sc, 2 sc in next sc) 7 times, sc in 4 sc—31 sts; turn.

Row 5: Ch 1, (sc2tog) 4 times, sc in each sc to last 8 sts, (sc2tog) 4 times—23 sts; turn.

Row 6: Ch 1, sc in each of first 10 sc, sc2tog, sc in last 11 sc—22 sts. Fasten off.

JOINING TOP TO SOLE

With WS of sole facing, find beg ch 3. Going backward, sk 2 hdc and 1 sc, mark next sc. Holding top to WS of sole, working through both lps on top and through front lps on sole (lp closest to top), join with sl st. Sl st around next 21 sts to join. Sl st in back lp of each of next 22 sts around sole; sl st in each rem back lp of sole (22 more sts).

BACK

Working in rem front lps around heel, ch 1, sc in 3 lps, hdc in 3 lps, dc in 10 lps, hdc in 3 lps, sc in 3 lps—22 sts; turn.

Row 2: Ch 1, sc in each st; turn.

Row 3: Ch 1, sc in 9 sc, (sc2tog) twice, sc in 9 sc; sk sl st row and next two sc rows on top, sl st after next sc row; turn.

Row 4: Sk sl st, sl st in each st around heel; sk sl st row and next two sc rows on top, sl st after next sc row; sl st across next seven sc rows on top; sl st to space above the first sc from Row 3.

Row 5: Ch 3 (counts as dc); working under the sl sts from Row 4, dc in each of next 19 sts; turn.

Row 6: Tie: Ch 50, sl st in first dc and in each of next 18 dc; in next dc (sl st, ch 50, sl st). Fasten off.

WEBS

Flatten top. With RS facing, join yarn with sl st in first sc row above sl st row, on Top next to side opening. Ch 1, sc in joining; (hdc in next st, 3 dc in next st, hdc in next st, sl st in next st) 4 times. Fasten off.

For second Duck Boot: Make as for the first up to the Webs. Sk first 6 sts; then work as for Webs on first Duck Boot.

Size It Right!

If the duck boots are too long for your baby, use a size 2/C (2.75mm) aluminum hook to make boots that are 3¼ in./8.2cm long or a size 1/B (2.25mm) hook to make boots that are 3 in./7.6mm long.

Tortoise Tracks

Bright colors in easy-care cotton yarn make striped zigzags over the body of this pullover, creating a whimsical look. Turtles, made separately and sewn on later, travel up the front.

MATERIALS

- Reynolds' Saucy Sport, 100% cotton (sport weight; distributed by JCA, Inc.), 1.75-oz./50g balls (each 123 yd./112m): 3 (3, 4, 4) skeins Turquoise #269 (A), 3 (3, 4, 4) skeins Royal Blue #255 (B), 2 (2, 2, 3) skeins Lime #63 (C)

- Size 3/D (3.25mm) aluminum crochet hook **or size needed to obtain gauge**

- Tapestry needle

GAUGE

- In Tracks Pattern: 20 sts = 4 in./10.2cm; 14 rows = 5 in./12.7cm

- In Sleeve Pattern: 18 sts and 13 rows = 4 in./10.2cm

SIZES

- For children, 2 (4, 6, 8); directions are written for the smallest size with changes for the larger sizes in parentheses

FINISHED MEASUREMENTS

- Finished Chest: 29 (31, 33½, 36) in./ 73.7 (78.7, 85.1, 91.4)cm

- Finished Length: 14½ (16, 17½, 19) in./ 36.9 (40.6, 44.5, 48,3)cm

ABBREVIATIONS

- sc2tog = draw up lp in each of next 2 sts, yo and draw through all 3 lps on hook

- dc2tog = (dc in next st until 2 lps rem on hook) twice, yo and draw through all 3 lps on hook

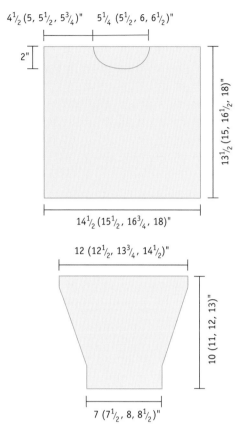

4$\frac{1}{2}$ (5, 5$\frac{1}{2}$, 5$\frac{3}{4}$)"   5$\frac{1}{4}$ (5$\frac{1}{2}$, 6, 6$\frac{1}{2}$)"

2"

13$\frac{1}{2}$ (15, 16$\frac{1}{2}$, 18)"

14$\frac{1}{2}$ (15$\frac{1}{2}$, 16$\frac{3}{4}$, 18)"

12 (12$\frac{1}{2}$, 13$\frac{3}{4}$, 14$\frac{1}{2}$)"

10 (11, 12, 13)"

7 (7$\frac{1}{2}$, 8, 8$\frac{1}{2}$)"

Before You Begin

- This pullover is worked using two colors on each pattern row. Carry the color not in use loosely along the top of the last row, working over it as you go.

- To change colors in double crochet: With the current color, work the double crochet until two loops remain on the hook; with the next color, yarn over and complete the double crochet.

- To change colors in single crochet: Draw up a loop with the current color; with the next color, complete the single crochet.

- Turn at the end of each row.

PATTERN STITCHES

Tracks Pattern

multiple of 6 sts; rep of 14 rows

Row 1 (RS): With A, ch 3 (counts as dc), dc in next sc; * dc in next 3 sc with B, dc in next 3 sc with A; rep from * across, ending dc in next 3 sc with B, dc in last sc with A, changing to B; turn.

Row 2: With B, ch 1, sc in first 3 dc; * sc in next 3 sts with A, sc in next 3 sts with B; rep from * across, ending sc in last 3 sts with A; turn.

Row 3: With A, ch 3 (counts as dc), dc in next 3 sc; * with B, dc in next 3 sc, with A, dc in next 3 sc; rep from * across, ending dc in last 2 sc with B; turn.

Row 4: With B, ch 1, sc in first dc; * with A, sc in next 3 sts; with B, sc in next 3 sts; rep from * across, ending sc in next 3 sts with A; sc in last 2 sts with B; turn.

Row 5: With B, ch 3 (counts as dc), dc in next 2 sts; * with A, dc in next 3 sts; with B, dc in next 3 sts; rep from * across, ending dc in last 3 sts with A, changing to B in last st; turn.

Row 6: With B, ch 1, sc in first dc; * with A, sc in next 3 sts; with B, sc in next 3 sts; rep from * across, ending sc in next 3 sts with A; sc in last 2 sts with B, changing to A; turn.

Row 7: Rep Row 3.

Row 8: With B, ch 1, sc in first 3 sts; * with A, sc in next 3 sts; with B, sc in next 3 sts; rep from * across, ending sc in last 3 sts with A; turn.

Row 9: Rep Row 1; *do not change to B in last st.*

Row 10: With A, ch 1, sc in first 2 sts; * with B, sc in next 3 sts; with A, sc in next 3 sts; rep from * across, ending sc in next 3 sts with B; sc in last st with A, changing to B; turn.

Row 11: With B, ch 3 (counts as dc), dc in next 2 sts; * with A, dc in next 3 sts; with B, dc in next 3 sts; rep from * across, ending dc in last 3 sts with A; turn.

Row 12: Rep Row 4.

Row 13: Rep Row 5; *do not change to B in last st.*

Row 14: Rep Row 10; *do not change to B in last st.*

Rep Rows 1 to 14 for Tracks Pattern.

SLEEVE PATTERN

multiple of any number of sts; rep of 2 rows

Row 1 (RS): Ch 3 (counts as dc); dc in each sc across; turn.

Row 2: Ch 1, sc in each dc across; turn.

Rep Rows 1 to 2 for Sleeve Pattern.

BACK

Beg at lower edge with B, ch 74 (80, 86, 92).

Foundation: Row 1: With B, dc in fourth ch from hook and in next ch. * With A, dc in next 3 ch; with B, dc in next 3 ch; rep from * across, ending dc in last 3 ch with A—72 (78, 84, 90) sts; turn.

Row 2: With A, ch 1, sc in first 2 dc; * with B, sc in next 3 dc; with A, sc in next 3 dc; rep from * across, ending sc in 3 dc with B; sc in last dc with A.

Beg Tracks Pattern, working even to approx 13½ (15, 16½, 18) in./34.3 (38.1, 41.9, 45.7)cm from beg, ending with WS row. Fasten off.

Lower Border: With RS facing, join C with sl st in lower right edge. Working in opposite edge of Foundation, sc in each rem ch across; turn. Work 5 more sc rows and fasten off.

FRONT

Work as for Back to approx 11½ (13, 14½, 16) in./ 29.2 (33, 37,9, 40.6)cm from beg, ending with WS row.

Left Shoulder: Work est pattern across first 25 (27, 29, 31) sts; turn, leaving rem sts unworked. Ch 1 with correct color, sk first sc, sc in color pattern across. Work one RS row across to last 3 sts, dc2tog, dc in last st; turn. Cont in pattern on rem 23 (25, 27, 29) sts to same length as Back. Fasten off.

Right Shoulder: With RS facing, sk center 22 (24, 26, 28) sts. Join correct color in next st with sl st, ch 3 (counts as dc). In est pattern, dc across; turn. Work one WS row across, ending sc2tog; turn. In color pattern, ch 3 (counts as dc), dc2tog; then cont to end of row. Cont in pattern on rem 23 (25, 27, 29) sts to same length as Back. Fasten off.

Lower Border: Work as for Back.

SLEEVES (make two)

Beg at lower edge with B, ch 34 (36, 38, 40).

Foundation Row 1: Dc in fourth ch from hook and in each ch across—32 (34, 36, 38) sts.

Row 2: Ch 1, sc in each dc across. Beg Sleeve Pattern, inc 1 st each edge every other row 9 (8, 9, 10) times then every fourth row 2 (3, 4, 4) times—54 (56, 62, 66) sts. *At the same time,* after working 8 (9, 10, 11) rows from the beg, change to A for 8 (9, 10, 11) rows. Then change to C and work even to approx 10 (11, 12, 13) in./25.4 (27.9, 30.5, 33)cm from beg, ending with WS row. Fasten off.

TORTOISE (make two)

Body

With C, ch 10.

Row 1 (RS): Sc in second ch from hook and in each ch across—9 sts; turn.

Row 2: Ch 1, sc in first sc; (tr in next sc, sc in next sc) across; turn.

Row 3: Ch 1, 2 sc in first sc; sc in each tr and sc across, ending 2 sc in last sc—11 sts; turn.

Row 4: Rep Row 2.

Row 5: Ch 1, sc in each sc and tr across; turn.

Row 6: Ch 1, sc in first 2 sc; (tr in next sc, sc in next sc) across, ending tr in next sc, sc in last 2 sc; turn.

Row 7: Rep Row 5.

Row 8: Sl st in first sc; (tr in next sc, sc in next sc) across, ending tr in next sc, sl st in last sc—9 sts; turn.

Row 9: Ch 1, sk sl st, sc in 9 sts; turn.

Row 10: Rep Row 8—7 sts; turn.

Appendages

First front foot: Ch 3, sc in second ch from hook, sc in next ch, sl st in sl st—first foot made. Sl st in next 2 sts.

For head: Sc in next 3 sts; turn. Ch 1, 2 sc in first sc, sc in next sc, 2 sc in last sc—5 sts; turn. Ch 1, sc2tog, sc in sc, sc2tog—3 sts; turn. Ch 1, draw up lp in each of next 3 sts, yo and draw through all 4 lps on hook. Fasten off.

Second front foot: With WS facing, join C with sl st in sl st at right edge; then complete as for First Front Foot.

First back foot: With RS facing, join C with sl st in first ch of Foundation. Ch 3, 2 sc in second ch from hook, sc in third ch, sl st in same ch as joining. Sl st in 3 ch.

For tail: In next ch (sl st, ch 3), sc in second ch from hook and in next ch, sl st in same ch as ch-3. Sl st in each of next 4 ch; turn.

Second back foot: Ch 3, 2 sc in second ch from hook, sc in third ch, sl st in last sl st. Fasten off.

Weave in loose ends on WS. Leave ends to add a bit of stuffing.

FINISHING

Join shoulder seams.

Place markers 6¼ (6½, 7, 7½) in./15.8 (16.5, 17.8, 19.1)cm each side of shoulder seams. Set in sleeves between markers.

Pin turtles onto front of sweater; with C, sew around body only.

Leaving lower borders on front and back free, join underarm and side seams, using matching yarns.

Sleeve Trim (make two): With RS facing, join B with sl st in seam. Sl st evenly around and fasten off.

Lower Trim: With RS facing, join C with sl st in any row along side vent. Sl st in each row and st around entire lower border. Fasten off.

Neckband: With RS facing, join C with sl st in left shoulder seam. Sl st evenly around neck—approx 64 (68, 72, 76) sts.

Rnd 2: Sc in back lp of each sl st around.

Rnds 3–4: Sc in back lp of each sc around. Fasten off.

A Different Look

Make more turtles and place them so they are following one another around the lower edge of the sweater, just above the border.

Costume Party

In my childhood room there was the most wonderful miniature picnic table made by my dad. I would gather my dolls around it and pretend that we were having a costume party, complete with beautiful things to wear. This section showcases real little dolls wearing beautiful garments.

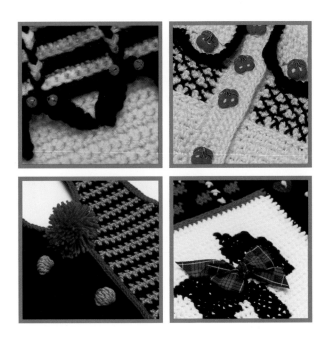

Baby Dress

● ●

Intermediate

Your own little Shirley Temple will look adorable in this sweet dress. A contrasting yarn color is used to work simple cross-stitch embroidery onto the single crochet bodice to simulate smocking. The garment buttons down the front so that dressing your baby will be easy.

MATERIALS

- J. & P. Coats Luster Sheen, Art. A95, 100% acrylic (machine-washable, sport weight), 1.8-oz./51g balls (each 150 yd./137.1m): 5 (5, 6, 6) balls Vanilla #7 (MC), 1 ball Black #2 (A)

- Size 3/D (3.25mm) aluminum crochet hook **or size needed to obtain gauge**

- Tapestry needle

- JHB International Buttons, ⅝ in./ 1.6cm long: 15 (15, 15, 16) Cherry Time #20200

GAUGE

- In Skirt Pattern: 26 sts and 22 rows = 4 in./10.2cm

- In Bodice Pattern: 20 sts and 20 rows = 4 in./10.2 cm

SIZES

- For babies, 3 (6, 9, 12) months; directions are written for the smallest size with changes for the larger sizes in parentheses

FINISHED MEASUREMENTS

- Chest (buttoned): 16¾ (18½, 19¾, 20¾) in./ 42.5 (47, 50.2, 52.7)cm
- Skirt (buttoned): 35½ (38½, 40¼, 41¾) in./ 90.2 (97.8, 102.2, 106)cm
- Length: 14¼ (14¾, 15¼, 15¾) in./36.2 (37.5, 38.7, 40)cm

ABBREVIATIONS

- sc2tog = draw up lp in each of next 2 sts, yo and draw through all 3 lps on hook
- sc3tog = draw up lp in each of next 3 sts, yo and draw through all 4 lps on hook

Before You Begin

- The cross-stitch embroidery, in black, is worked after the crocheting has been completed.
- Turn at the end of each row.

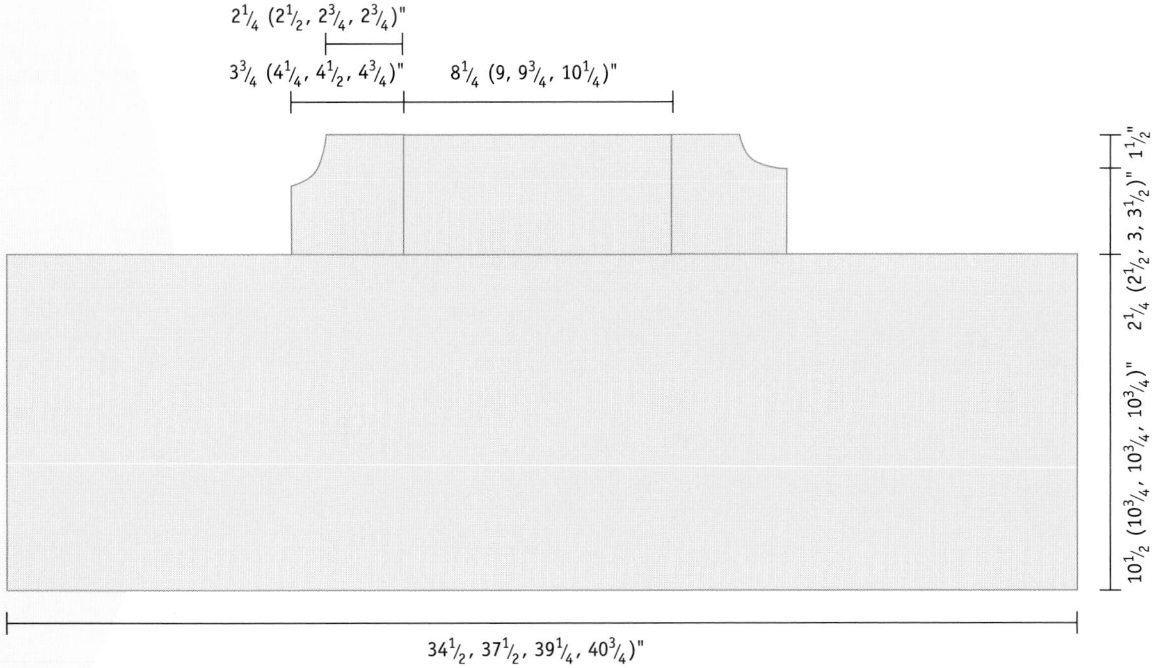
2¼ (2½, 2¾, 2¾)"
3¾ (4¼, 4½, 4¾)"
8¼ (9, 9¾, 10¼)"
1½"
2¼ (2½, 3, 3½)"
10½ (10¾, 10¾, 10¾)"
34½, 37½, 39¼, 40¾)"

BODICE EMBROIDERY PATTERN

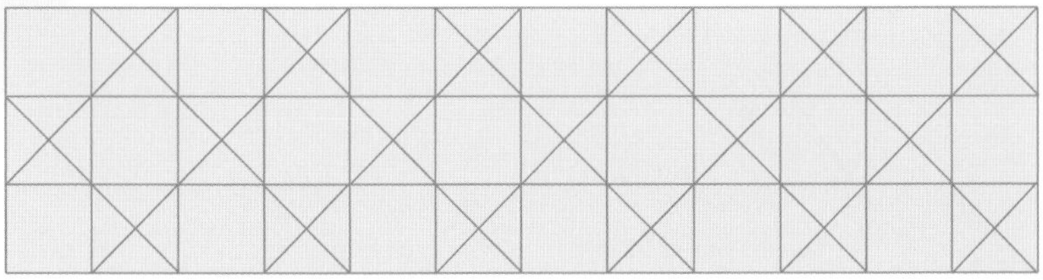

PATTERN STITCHES
Skirt Pattern
multiple of 2 sts + 1 st; rep of 2 rows

Row 1 (RS): Ch 1, sc in sc; (ch 1, sk 1 sc, sc in next ch-1 sp) across, ending ch 1, sk 1 sc, sc in last sc; turn.

Row 2: Ch 1, sc in sc and ch-1 sp; (ch 1, sk 1 sc, sc in next ch-1 sp) across, ending sc in last sc; turn.

Rep Rows 1 to 2 for Skirt Pattern.

Bodice Pattern
any multiple; 1 row rep

Ch 1, sc in each sc across; turn.

SKIRT
Beg at lower edge with MC, ch 226 (244, 256, 266).

Foundation, Row 1 (RS): Sc in second ch from hook; (ch 1, sk 1 ch, sc in next ch) across—225 (243, 255, 265) sts; turn.

Row 2: Ch 1, sc in sc and ch-1 sp; (ch 1, sk 1 sc, sc in next ch-1 sp) across, ending sc in last sc; turn.

Cont in Skirt Pattern to approx 9½ (10, 10, 10) in./ 24.2 (25.4, 25.4, 25.4)cm from beg, ending with WS row.

Skirt Shaping: Sc in first 3 (5, 8, 8) sc; (sc3tog) across, ending sc in last 3 (4, 7, 8) sc—79 (87, 95, 99) sts; turn.

For waistband: Ch 1, sl st in back lp of each st across; turn. Ch 1, working in rem lps, sc in each lp across.

LEFT FRONT
Row 1 (WS): Ch 1, sc in first 19 (21, 23, 24) sc; turn.

Cont in sc until bodice measures approx 2¼ (2½, 3, 3½) in./5.7 (6.4, 7.6, 8.9)cm from beg, ending with WS row.

Neck Shaping: Sc across, leaving last 5 (6, 7, 8) sts unworked—14 (15, 16, 16) sts; turn. Ch 1, sc2tog, sc in each sc across; turn. Ch 1, sc in each sc across, ending sc2tog; turn.

Cont in sc on rem 12 (13, 14, 14) sts until bodice measures approx 3¾ (4, 4½, 5) in./9.5 (10.2, 11.4, 12.7)cm from beg. Fasten off.

BACK
With WS facing, join MC with sl st in st next to left front. Ch 1, sc in same st as joining and in each of next 40 (44, 48, 50) sts; turn. Cont in Bodice Pattern on 41 (45, 49, 51) sts to same length as left front. Fasten off.

RIGHT FRONT
With WS facing, join MC with sl st in st next to back. Ch 1, sc in same st as joining and in each of rem sts. Work as for Left Front on 19 (21, 23, 24) sts, reversing Neck Shaping.

SLEEVES (make two)
Beg at lower edge, with MC, ch 33 (35, 39, 43).

Row 1 (RS): Sc in second ch from hook and in each ch across—32 (34, 38, 42) sts; turn.

Row 2: Ch 1, 2 sc in each sc across—64 (68, 76, 84) sts; turn.

Row 3: Ch 1, sc in first 10 sc, hdc across, ending sc in last 10 sc; turn.

Row 4: Sl st in first 5 sc; sc in each st across, leaving last 5 sc unworked; turn.

Row 5: Sl st in first 5 sc, sc in next 5 sc, hdc across, ending sc in 5 sc and leaving last 5 sc unworked— 44 (48, 56, 64) sts; turn.

Row 6: Ch 1, sc in each st across; turn.

Row 7: Ch 1, sc in first 5 sc, hdc across, ending sc in last 5 sc; turn.

Row 8: Ch 1, sc2tog, sc in each st across, ending sc2tog; turn.

Row 9: Ch 1, sc2tog, sc in next 2 sc, hdc across to last 4 sts, sc in 2 sc, sc2tog; turn.

Row 10: Rep Row 8.

Row 11: Ch 1, sc2tog, hdc in each st across, ending sc2tog; turn.

Rows 12–13: Rep Rows 10 to 11. After Row 13— 32 (36, 44, 52) sts.

Row 14: Ch 1, sk 1 (0, 1, 0), (sc3tog) across, ending sk 1 (0, 1, 1) st. Fasten off.

Join sleeve seam. With RS facing, join A with sl st in seam. Ch 1, sc in each rem ch from foundation around. Sl st in back lp of each sc around. Join and fasten off.

FINISHING

Join shoulder seams. Distributing sleeve cap fullness over shoulder area, set in sleeves.

Buttonhole Band: With RS facing, join MC with sl st in lower right front edge. Ch 1, work 65 (67, 67, 67) sc evenly spaced to bodice; work 14 (15, 17, 19) sc evenly spaced along bodice to neck edge; turn. Ch 1, sc in each sc across; turn. Ch 1, sc in first 12 (13, 13, 13) sc; (ch 2, sk 2 sc, sc in next 7 sc) 6 times, [ch 2, sk 2 sc, sc in next 3 (4, 5, 6) sc] twice, ch 2, sk 2 sc, sc in last sc; turn. Ch 1, sc in each sc across, working 2 sc in each ch-2 sp; turn. Work one more sc row and fasten off.

Button Band: With RS facing, join MC with sl st at neck edge on left front. Ch 1, work 14 (15, 17, 19) sc evenly spaced along bodice and 65 (67, 67, 67) sc evenly spaced to lower edge; turn. Work 4 more sc rows and fasten off.

Sew buttons opposite buttonholes.

Collar

With RS facing, join MC with sl st in top edge of button-hole band. Sl st across first four rows of band, sc in next row. Work 15 (16, 17, 18) sc evenly spaced to shoulder, 19 (21, 23, 25) sts evenly spaced along back neck, 15 (16, 17, 18) sc evenly spaced to left band, and 1 sc in first row of band—51 (55, 59, 63) sc; turn.

Row 2: Ch 1, sc in first 1 (3, 5, 7) sc; * 2 sc in next sc, sc in next 5 sc; rep from * across 7 times more, 2 sc in next sc, sc in last 1 (3, 5, 7) sc; turn.

Row 3: Ch 1, sc in each sc across—60 (64, 68, 72) sts; turn.

Row 4: Ch 1, sc in first 1 (3, 5, 7) sc; * 2 sc in next sc, sc in next 6 sc; rep from * across 7 times more, 2 sc in next sc, sc in each rem sc across; turn.

Row 5: Rep Row 3—69 (73, 77, 81) sts; turn.

Row 6: Ch 1, sc in first 2 (4, 3, 2) sc; * sk 2 sc, 7 dc in next sc, sk 2 sc, sc in next sc; rep from * across, ending sk 2 sc, 7 dc in next sc, sk 2 sc, sc in last 2 (4, 3, 2) sc—11 (11, 12, 13) shells. Fasten off.

Row 7: With the RS facing, join A with sl st in side of collar near button band. Ch 1, sc in same sp as joining, sc evenly along side, sc in each st across collar, sc evenly along opposite side. Fasten off.

CROSS-STITCH EMBROIDERY

Step 1   Step 2   Step 3   Step 4

Row 8: With RS facing, join A with sl st in first sc. (Ch 1, sl st in next sc) across for rickrack trim, ending at opposite edge of collar. Fasten off.

* Sew 1 button in first 7-dc-shell; (sk 1 shell, sew 1 button onto next shell) twice *. Beg at opposite edge, rep from * to *. For size 12 months, sew 1 button onto center back shell.

Lower Edge: With RS facing, join MC with sl st in corner of lower left button band. Ch 1, work 5 sc across band. Working along rem ch from Foundation, sc in 2 (2, 2, 1) ch; * sk 2 ch, 5 dc in next ch, sk 2 ch, sc in next ch; rep from * across, ending sc in 1 (1, 1, 0) ch, 5 sc across band. Fasten off.

With the RS facing, join MC with sl st in first sc at left edge. (Ch 1, sl st in next st) across for rickrack edging. At end, fasten off.

Embroidery

Thread tapestry needle with 18-in./45.7cm strand of A. With RS of back facing, and leaving a 3-in./7.6cm tail to weave in later, beg cross-stitching in second sc row above band and in closest sc next to right edge as follows:

Step 1: Bring threaded needle from back to front at lower left end of first sc; then take to WS at upper right end of first sc, as shown above.

Step 2: Bring needle from back to front at left upper end of first sc; then take to WS at lower right end of first sc.

Step 3: Sk next sc to the left. Rep Step 1.

Step 4: Rep Step 2 to complete the next cross-stitch.

Rep Steps 3 and 4 across entire back. Leaving a 3-in./ 7.6cm tail to weave in later, cut yarn. For the next row, make cross-stitches in the sc above the skipped sc in first row (see "Bodice Embroidery Pattern" on p. 47). Rep for 7 total rows.

Add cross-stitch rows to right and left front. Weave in tails on WS of fabric and secure in place.

A Different Look

If you find you enjoy the cross-stitch embroidery, go ahead and fill the entire bodice with it. On the other hand, if making little stitches on a crocheted dress is not your bag, sew some black rickrack to the bodice above the band to add a little zest.

Bats!

● ●

Tiny red jingle bells light up the eyes
of each bat on the sweater front.
The batwing sleeves, worked directly
onto the garment, and the vented
sides allow for plenty of room for
growth. What girl wouldn't love
the matching doll sweater?

*Advanced
Beginner*

MATERIALS

Girl's Sweater

- Patons' Astra, 100% acrylic (sport weight;
  distributed by Spinrite Inc.), 1.75-oz./
  50g balls (each 178 yd./163m):
  3 (4, 5, 6) balls School Bus Yellow
  #2941 (A)

- Patons' Look at Me!, 60% acrylic/
  40% nylon (sport weight; distributed
  by Spinrite Inc.), 1.75-oz./50g balls
  (152 yd./138.9m): 2 (3, 3, 3) balls
  Happy Days Variegated #6376 (B),
  2 (3, 3, 3,) balls Black #6364 (C)

- Size 5/F (4.00mm) aluminum crochet hook
  or size needed to obtain gauge

- Tapestry needle

- JHB International Buttons, ⅝ in./
  1.6cm long: 4 Coeur D'Alene
  #40092 (red)

- Sewing needle

- Black sewing thread

- Darice Bells, ¼ in./6mm: 12 (14, 16,
  18) Red Jingle Bells

Doll's Sweater

- Astra: ½ ball School Bus Yellow #2941

- Look at Me!: scraps Happy Days Variegated #6376 and Black #6364

The Set

- Astra: 4 (5, 6, 7) balls School Bus Yellow #2941

- Look at Me!: 2 (3, 3, 3) balls Happy Days Variegated #6376, 2 (3, 3, 3,) balls Black #6364)

GAUGE

- In Striped Pattern: 20 sts = 5 in./12.7cm; 14 rows = 3 in./7.6cm

- In sc: 16 sts and 19 rows = 4 in./10.2cm

SIZES

Girl's Sweater

- For children, 4 (6, 8, 10); directions are written for the smallest size with changes for the larger sizes in parentheses

Doll's Sweater

- For an 18-in./45.7cm doll

FINISHED MEASUREMENTS

Girl's Sweater

- Chest: 27½ (31½, 35½, 39½) in./67.9 (80, 99.2, 100.4)cm

- Length: 15 (17, 18½, 20) in./38.1 (43.2, 47, 52.1)cm

Doll's Sweater

- Chest: 9¼ in./23.5cm

- Length: 7 in./17.8cm

ABBREVIATIONS

- fpdc = front post double crochet: yo, insert hook from front to back then to front to go around dc post, draw up lp, (yo and draw through 2 lps on hook) twice

- fpdc over fpdc = on RS, fpdc over fpdc 2 rows below, skipping sc behind new st; on WS, sc in top of fpdc

- MB = make bobble: sl st in back lp of next st, in same st [(yo and draw up lp, yo and draw through 2 lps on hook) 4 times, yo and draw through all 5 lps on hook, ch 1 to close], sl st in back lp of same st

- sc2tog = draw up lp in each of next 2 sts, yo and draw through all 3 lps on hook

●●●●●●●●●○○

Before You Begin

- The back and front of the girl's sweater are constructed by working from the neck to the lower edge. The shoulder and neck shapings are added before the shoulders are joined. Finally, the batwing sleeves are worked onto the striped portion of the upper body.

- While working the Striped Pattern, carry the color not in use loosely along the side edge.

- Turn at the end of each row.

PATTERN STITCH

Striped Pattern

multiple of 8 sts + 7 sts; rep of 4 rows

Row 1 (RS): Working in back lps with B, ch 1, sc in each of first 7 sc; * fpdc over fpdc, sc in back lps of next 7 sc; rep from * across; turn.

Row 2: Working through both lps with B, ch 1, sc in each st across; turn.

Row 3: With C, rep Row 1.

Row 4: With C, rep Row 2.

Rep Rows 1 to 4 for Striped Pattern.

● Girl's Sweater ●

BACK

Beg at neck with C, ch 56 (64, 72, 80).

Foundation Row 1 (RS): Sc in second ch from hook and in each of next 6 ch; * dc in next ch, sc in each of next 7 ch; rep from * across—55 (63, 71, 79) sts; turn.

Row 2: Ch 1, sc in each sc and dc across; turn.

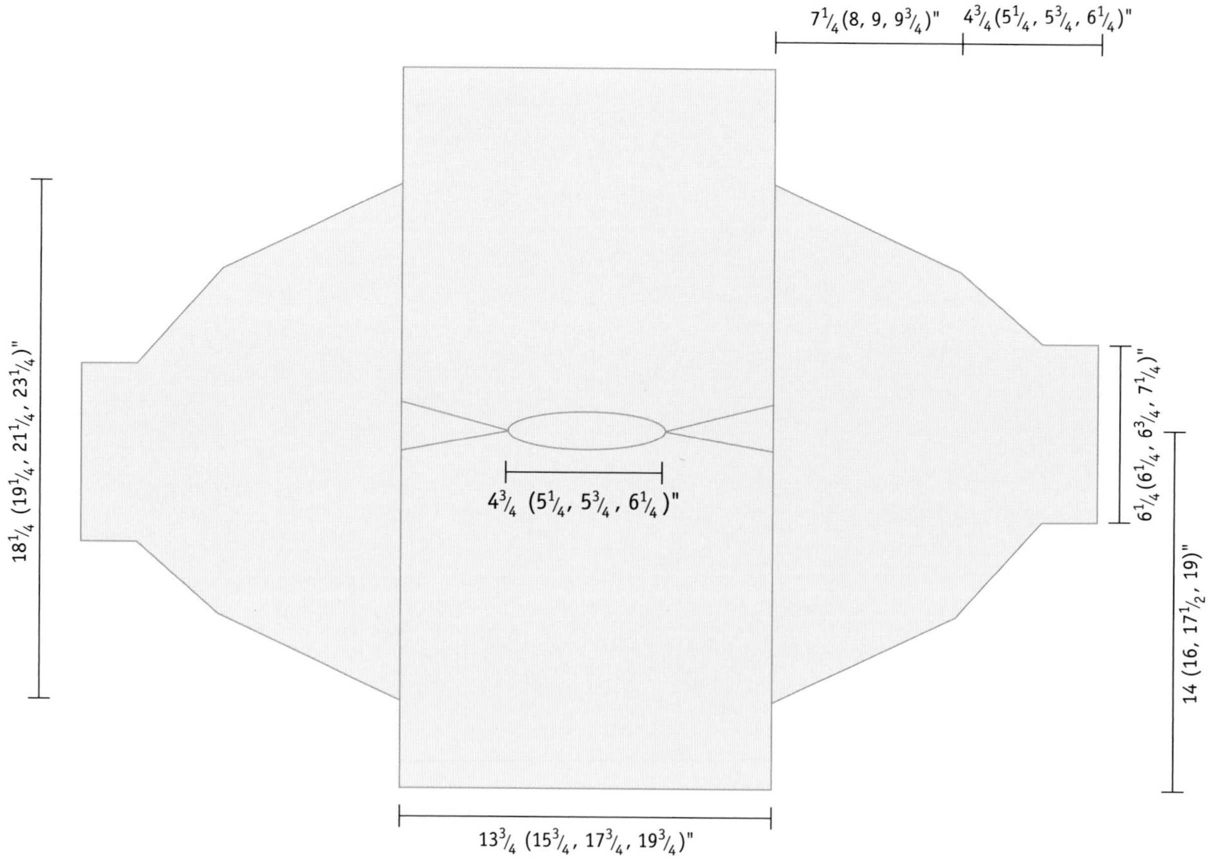
7¼ (8, 9, 9¾)"
4¾ (5¼, 5¾, 6¼)"
18¼ (19¼, 21¼, 23¼)"
4¾ (5¼, 5¾, 6¼)"
6¼ (6¼, 6¾, 7¼)"
14 (16, 17½, 19)"
13¾ (15¾, 17¾, 19¾)"

Row 3: With RS facing, join B with sl st in back lp of first st. Ch 1, working in back lps, sc in same lp as joining and in each of next 6 lps. * Fpdc over dc from Row 1, sc in back lp of next 7 sc; rep from * across; turn.

Row 4: With B, sc in each st across; turn.

Rows 5–6: With C, rep Rows 3 to 4.

Upper Body: Beg Striped Pattern and cont as est to approx 7 (7½, 8¼, 9) in./17.8 (20.1, 20.9, 22.9)cm from beg, ending with Row 3.

Bats: With C, ch 1, sc in back lp of each sc across, making a Bat in each fpdc as follows: **For Wings and Head:** * Sl st in back lp of st, ch 7. Sc in second ch from hook and next ch, hdc in next 2 ch, dc in next 2 ch, sl st in back lp of root stitch **, MB, sl st in root st, rep from * to ** for second wing. Fasten off B and C.

With RS facing, join A in first rem lp. Ch 1, sc in each sc across working sc under each Bat—55 (63, 71, 79) sts. Cont in sc with A to approx 14 (16, 17½, 19) in./ 35.6 (40.6, 44,5, 48.3)cm from beg. Fasten off.

Shoulders: With RS facing, and working along rem Foundation ch, join C with sl st in first rem ch at top right edge. Ch 1, sc in same ch as joining and in each of next 5 (6, 7, 8) ch, hdc in next 6 (7, 8, 9) ch, dc in next 6 (7, 8, 9) ch. Fasten off.

Sk center 19 (21, 23, 25) ch for neck opening. Join C in next ch, ch 3 (counts as dc). Dc in each of next 5 (6, 7, 8) ch, hdc in next 6 (7, 8, 9) ch, sc in last 6 (7, 8, 9) ch. Fasten off.

FRONT

Work as for Back

Shoulder Joining: Sew last 6 (7, 8, 9) sc at each edge tog for shoulder seam.

Left Shoulder: With RS facing and beg on back, join C with sl st in first dc. Sl st in next dc, ch 2, sk 2 sts, sl st in next 3 sts, ch 2, sk 2 sts, sl st in each rem st around. Fasten off.

Right Shoulder: With RS facing and beg on Front, sl st in each st around opening to last 9 sts. Ch 2, sk 2 sts, sl st in next 3 sts, ch 2, sk 2 sts, sl st in last 2 sts and fasten off.

Sew buttons opposite buttonholes.

SLEEVES (make two, reversing one)

With RS facing, join C with sl st in last black stripe on upper body of front. Ch 1, work 73 (77, 85, 93) sc evenly spaced to last black stripe on back; turn.

Row 2: Ch 1, sc2tog, sc in each sc across, ending sc2tog—71 (75, 83, 91) sts.

Row 3: With B, working in back lps, sc in each of first 19 (21, 21, 21) sts; (dc in next st, sc in next 7 sts) for 4 (4, 5, 6) times, dc in next st, sc in each of last 19 (21, 21, 21) sts; turn.

Row 4: Ch 1, working through both lps, sc2tog, sc in each sc across, ending sc2tog—69 (73, 81, 89) sts; turn.

Row 5: With C, working in back lps, sc in 18 (20, 20, 20) sts; * fpdc over dc from Row 3, sc in each of next 7 sc; rep from * across for 3 (3, 4, 5) times more. Fpdc over dc from Row 3, sc in last 18 (20, 20, 20) sts; turn.

Dec 1 st each edge every other row, work in Striped Pattern until there are 8 (9, 10, 11) stripes in B and 9 (10, 11, 12) stripes in C. Sleeve should measure approx 7¼ (8, 9, 9¾) in./18.4 (20.3, 22.9, 23.5)cm long with 39 (39, 43, 47) sts rem.

Change to A. Sc through both lps of every row, dec 1 st each edge every row until 25 (25, 27, 29) sts rem.

For cuff, cont in sc until sleeve measures approx 12 (12½, 13¼, 14) in./30.5 (31.8, 33.6, 35.6). Fasten off.

FINISHING

Join sleeve seams with matching colors. Turn back cuffs.

Lower Body Edging: With RS facing, join A with sl st at top edge of one side, right below sleeve. Ch 1, work * 33 (40, 43, 47) sc evenly spaced along side. In corner (sc, ch 1, sc), sc in each sc across, working (sc, ch 1, sc) in corner, 33 (40, 43, 47) sc evenly spaced along next side **. Rep from * to ** for opposite side. * Sl st in each of first 6 sc, sc in 8 sc, hdc in 10 sc, dc in 9 (16, 19, 23) sc. 3 dc in corner ch-1 sp, dc in each sc across, working 3 dc in next corner ch-1 sp. Dc in 9 (16, 19, 23) sc, hdc in 10 sc, sc in 8 sc, sl st in 6 sc **. Rep from * to ** for opposite side. Sl st in each st around and fasten off.

With A, sew from top of vent down 3 in./7.6cm.

Embellishments: Thread sewing needle with black thread. Sew red bells to each side of Bats' heads on front only.

• Doll's Sweater •

BACK

Beg at neck with C, ch 24. Rep Foundation Rows as for Girl's Sweater Back—23 sts. Rep Striped Pattern, Rows 1 to 4; then rep Rows 1–3. Make Bats. Fasten off B and C.

With RS facing, join A in first rem lp. Ch 1, sc in each sc across working a sc under each bat—23 sts. Cont in sc with A to approx 6½ in./16.5cm from beg. Fasten off.

Shoulders: With RS facing, join C with sl st in first rem ch of Foundation. Ch 1, sc in same ch, sc in next ch, hdc in each of next 2 ch, dc in each of next 2 ch. Fasten off. Sk center 11 ch. With RS facing, join C with sl st in next rem ch of Foundation. Ch 3 (counts as dc), dc in next ch, hdc in each of next 2 ch, sc in last 2 ch. Fasten off.

FRONT

Work as for Back. Join shoulder seams.

SLEEVES (make two)

With RS facing, join C with sl st in side of last color stripe. Ch 1, sc in same row as joining; work 30 sc evenly spaced to opposite color row—31 sts. Dec 1 st each edge every row until 21 sts rem work Sleeve Pattern as follows.

A Different Look

For a boy, leave off the batwing sleeves and make a vest instead. Then sew the side seams up, leaving 5½ (6, 6½, 7) in./14 (15.2, 16.5, 17.8)cm open at the top for the armholes. If you wish, use black yarn to slip stitch or single crochet evenly around the opening.

Row 1: Ch 1, sc in both lps of each sc across with C; turn.

Row 2: Ch 1, in back lps with B, sc in each sc across; turn.

Row 3: Ch 1, in both lps with B, sc in each sc across; turn.

Row 4: Ch 1, in back lps with C, sc in each sc across; turn.

Rep Rows 1 to 4, twice; then rep Row 1 again. Change to A and work in sc for 7 rows. Fasten off.

FINISHING

With RS facing, join C with sl st near shoulder seam. Ch 1, work 32 sc evenly spaced around neck. Sl st in first sc; (ch 1, sl st in next sc) around for rickrack trim. At end, ch 1 and fasten off. Hide tail.

Join underarm and side seam to bottom of last black stripe.

Lower Edging: With RS facing, join A with sl st in any corner at lower edge. Ch 1, sc evenly around, working 2 sc in each corner. Rep rickrack trim as for neck, sk 1 sc at top of each vent.

Clown Romper

• •

Intermediate

Fastening the leg openings will be a "snap" when it's time to change your little clown's nappy. The two pieces of this easy romper are joined together with mattress stitching through a slip-stitch border.

MATERIALS

- Stylecraft-Satin Touch, 100% acrylic (DK weight; distributed by S. R. Kertzer) 3.5-oz./100g skeins (each 248 yd./233m): 1 (1, 1, 2, 2) skeins Jet #1378 (MC), 1 skein Bluebird #1394 (A), 1 skein Ruby #1379 (B)

- Size 5/F (4.00mm) aluminum crochet hook **or size needed to obtain gauge**

- Size 3/D (3.25mm) aluminum crochet hook

- Tapestry needle

- Dritz Snap Tape: 1 (1, 1, 1, 2) packages Black

GAUGE

- In Body Pattern: 20 sts and 16 rows = 4 in./10.2cm

SIZES

- For babies, 3 (6, 9, 12, 18) months; directions are written for the smallest size with changes for the larger sizes in parentheses

FINISHED MEASUREMENTS

- Chest: 18½ (20, 21½, 23¼, 24¾) in./ 47 (50.8, 54.9, 59, 62.9)cm

- Hips: 11¾ (12½, 13, 13¾, 15) in./ 29.8 (31.8, 33, 34.9, 38.1)cm

- Length: 21 (22, 22¾, 24, 25) in./ 53.3 (55.9, 57.8, 61, 63.5)cm

ABBREVIATION

- sc2tog = draw up lp in each of next 2 sts, yo and draw through all 3 lps on hook

● ● ● ● ● ● ● ● ○ ○ ○

Before You Begin

- To change colors at the end of a row: In the last stitch, draw up a loop with the current color; with the next color, complete the stitch. Carry unused strand loosely along edge.
- Note that the cuff is added after the leg has been completed.
- Turn at the end of each row.

PATTERN STITCHES

Striped Body Pattern

multiple of 2 sts + 1 st; rep of 4 rows

Row 1 (RS): With A, ch 1, sc in first sc; * ch 1, sk 1 sc, sc in next ch-1 sp; rep from * across, ending ch 1, sk 1 sc, sc in last sc; turn.

Row 2: With A, ch 1, sc in first sc, sc in ch-1 sp; * ch 1, sk 1 sc, sc in next ch-1 sp; rep from * across, ending sc in last sc changing to MC; turn.

Rows 3–4: With MC, rep Rows 1 to 2. In last sc of Row 4, change to A.

Rep Rows 1 to 4 for Striped Pattern.

Solid Body Pattern

With MC, rep Rows 1 to 2 of Striped Body Pattern.

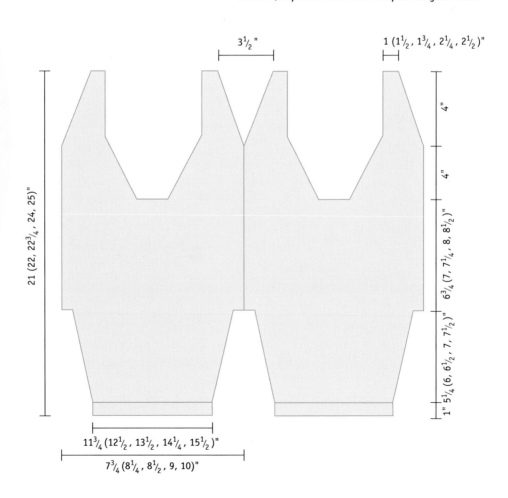

Row 2: Ch 1, sc in first sc, sc in ch-1 sp; * ch 1, sk 1 sc, sc in next ch-1 sp; rep from * across, ending sc in last sc and change to A; turn.

Rep Striped Body Pattern Rows 1 to 2.

Inc Row 1 (RS): With MC, ch 1, 2 sc in first sc; * ch 1, sk 1 sc, sc in next ch-1 sp; rep from * across, ending ch 1, sk 1 sc, 2 sc in last sc; turn.

Cont in pattern, inc 1 st each edge every other row 4 (6, 6, 8, 10) times; then inc 1 st each edge every row 3 (2, 3, 2, 1) times—55 (59, 63, 67, 73) sts. Work even to approx 5¼ (6, 6½, 7, 7½) in./13.3 (15.2, 16.5, 17.8, 19.1)cm from beg.

Crotch Shaping: At beg of next two rows, ch 3. Sc in second ch from hook, sc in next ch; cont est pattern across row. Cont in Striped Body Pattern on 59 (63, 67, 71, 77) sts to approx 12 (13, 13¾, 15, 16) in./30.5 (33, 34.9, 38.1, 40.6)cm from beg, ending with RS row.

Armhole Shaping (Back Section of first piece): Work est pattern across first 23 (25, 27, 29, 31) sts; turn, leaving rem sts for later. **Dec Row:** Work in pattern across to last 2 sts (either 2 sc or ch-1 sp and 1 sc), sc2tog over last 2 sts. Dec 1 st at armhole edge every other row 4 times, then every row 4 times. Cont in pattern on rem 14 (16, 18, 20, 22) sts to approx 16 (17, 17¾, 19, 20) in./40.6 (43.2, 45.1, 48.3, 50.8)cm from beg.

Neck Shaping: Dec 1 st at neck edge (sc2tog over 2 sc or ch-1 and 1 sc) every other row 5 times, then every row 4 times. Cont in pattern on rem 5 (7, 9, 11, 13) sts to approx 20 (21, 21¾, 23, 24) in./50.8 (53.3, 55.2, 58.4, 61)cm from beg. Fasten off.

Front Section of first piece: With WS facing, sk 13 (13, 13, 13, 15) sts. Join appropriate yarn with sl st in next sc. Ch 1, sc in same sc as joining. Work in pattern to end of row. Complete as for Back Section.

SECOND LEG

Working entire piece with MC, complete as for First Leg, using Solid Body Pattern.

FIRST LEG

Beg at lower edge, with MC and larger hook, ch 40 (42, 44, 46, 50).

Foundation, Row 1 (RS): Sc in second ch from hook; * ch 1, sk 1 ch, sc in next ch; rep from * across— 39 (41, 43, 45, 49) sts; turn.

Tip for Success

To determine bobble placement, use safety pins to mark the locations. Then look to see if your scheme is pleasing before you add the bobbles.

CUFFS (make two)

Working from side to side with B and smaller hook, ch 12. Sc in second ch from hook and in each ch across—11 sts; turn.

Row 2: Ch 1, sc in back lp of each sc across; turn.

Rep Row 2 until Cuff measures approx 7¾ (8¼, 8½, 9, 10) in./19.7 (20.9, 21.6, 22.9, 25.4)cm from beg. Fasten off.

FINISHING

Using MC, join striped shoulders; then join solid shoulders.

Joining Body

For Front: With RS facing, using B and larger hook, beg at first Neck Shaping row on striped section and sl st to crotch—1 sl st per row; then beg at crotch on solid piece, make 1 sl st per row to V-neck. **Rnd 2:** Sl st in each lp that is farther from center Front around. **Rnd 3:** Sl st in each rem lp around. Leaving an 18-in./45.7cm tail for sewing, fasten off.

Thread tapestry needle with tail and join pieces through back lps of the last sl st rnd.

For Back: Work as for Front, with first sl st row beg on solid side.

Neck Edging: With RS facing using B and larger hook, beg at shoulder seam and work 1 sl st per row around, working 1 sl st in center of each joining section. **Rnd 2:** Sl st in each front lp around. **Rnd 3:** Sl st in each back lp around and fasten off.

Armhole Edging (make two): With RS facing using B and larger hook, beg at center of underarm. Sl st evenly around. Rep Rnds 2 and 3 of Neck Edging.

Bobbles: With RS of Front facing, make 8 randomly placed bobbles with A as follows: On solid side, join A in skipped sc with sl st. Ch 4 (counts as tr), keeping last lp of each tr on hook, work 6 tr in same sc as joining, yo and draw through all 7 lps on hook. Ch 1 to close and fasten off. Take ends to WS near bobble base; secure in place.

Cuffs: Holding WS of cuff to RS of leg, using B and larger hook, sl st across to join. Rep for second cuff. Fold cuff in half toward RS of leg. With RS facing, using MC and larger hook, sl st evenly across first folded cuff, 1 sl st per row along leg, 1 sl st in seam, 1 sl st per row along second leg, sl st evenly to fold on second cuff. Fasten off. With RS facing, join MC in first sl st, ch 1, sc in each sl st around; turn. Work 3 more sc rows and fasten off.

Folding raw edges under, baste snap tape to RS of each sc leg band, making certain that snaps will match. Carefully machine or hand stitch tapes securely in place with black thread. Snap tapes tog. Sew bands to WS of cuffs.

Pompom: Wrap B around a credit card 50 times. Slip lps off card. With separate strand of yarn; tie all lps tog tightly in center. Cut lps at each end; trim. Sew or pin pompom onto front neck edge at center.

Highlander

● ●

Intermediate

The addition of yellow cross-stitch embroidery creates a plaid on portions of this cardigan. The Scotties are also worked with cross-stitches. Tie some plaid ribbon about the pups' necks for fun and be sure to purchase enough to make a matching hair bow for your child!

MATERIALS

- Dale's Kolibri, 100% cotton (machine-washable, sport weight), 1.75-oz./ 50g skeins (each 114 yd./105m):
  3 (3, 4, 4) skeins of Black #0090 (A),
  4 (4, 5, 5) skeins Red #3808 (B),
  1 (1, 2, 2) skeins White #0010 (C),
  1 (1, 1, 1) skein Yellow #2208 (D)

- Size 4/E (3.5mm) aluminum crochet hook
  or size needed to obtain gauge

- Yarn needle

- JHB International Buttons, ¾ in./1.9cm in diameter:
  5 Plaid Heart #20368

- Plaid ribbon, 1⅜-in./3.5cm wide: 1 yd./0.91m
  Red/Black/Yellow

GAUGE

- In sc and color pattern: 28 sts = 6 in./15.2cm;
  16 rows = 4 in./10.2cm

- In Body Pattern: 20 sts = 5 in./12.7cm;
  11 rows = 3 in./7.6cm

SIZES

- For girls, 2 (4, 6, 8); directions are written for the smallest size with changes for the larger sizes in parentheses

FINISHED MEASUREMENTS

- Chest (buttoned): 28 (30, 33, 36) in./71.1 (76.2, 83.3, 91.4)cm

- Length: 13½ (15½, 17½, 19½) in./34.3 (39.4, 44.5, 49.6)cm

ABBREVIATION

- sc2tog = draw up lp in each of next 2 sts, yo and draw through all 3 lps on hook

●●●●●●●●●●●○○

Before You Begin

- The Plaid Pattern is worked in single crochet from a chart, which is read from right to left for the right side rows and from left to right for the wrong side rows.

- The X's on the Plaid Pattern chart indicate embroidered cross-stitches, which are worked with yellow yarn after the crocheting has been completed.

- The Scottie's are cross-stitched in black yarn after the crocheting has been completed.

- To change colors in single crochet: Draw up a loop with the current color; with the next color, complete the single crochet.

- Turn at the end of each row.

PATTERN STITCHES

Body Pattern

Row 1: With WS facing join B with sl st in first sc. Ch 1, sc in joining and in each sc across.

Row 2: With B, ch 1, hdc in each sc across.

Row 3: With B, ch 1, sc in each hdc across.

Row 4: Rep Row 2.

Row 5: With RS facing, join A with sl st in first hdc. Ch 1, sc in joining and in each hdc across. Fasten off.

Rep Rows 1 to 5 for Body Pattern.

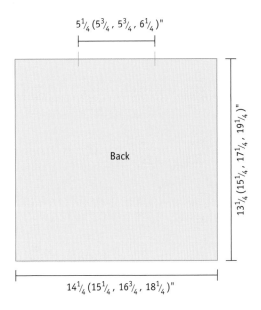

5¼ (5¾, 5¾, 6¼)"

Back

13½ (15½, 17½, 19½)"

14¼ (15¼, 16¾, 18¼)"

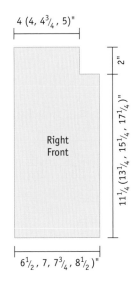

4 (4, 4¾, 5)"

2"

Right Front

11½ (13½, 15¼, 17¼)"

6½, 7, 7¾, 8½)"

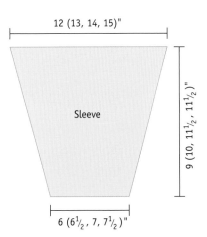

12 (13, 14, 15)"

Sleeve

9 (10, 11½, 11½)"

6 (6½, 7, 7½)"

PLAID PATTERN

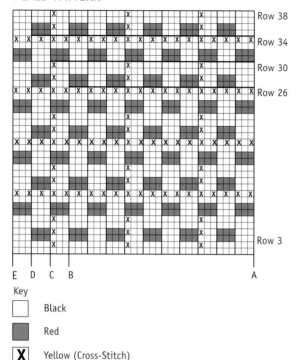

Row 38
Row 34
Row 30
Row 26

Row 3

E D C B   A

Key

☐ Black

▨ Red

☒ Yellow (Cross-Stitch)

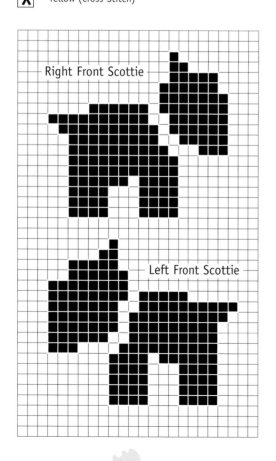

Right Front Scottie

Left Front Scottie

BACK

Beg at lower edge with A, ch 58 (62, 68, 74).

Foundation (RS): Sc in second ch from hook and in each ch across—57 (61, 67, 73) sts. Fasten off.

Beg Body Pattern, rep Rows 1 to 5 to approx 13¼ (15¼, 17¼, 19¼) in./33.6 (38.7, 43.8, 48.9)cm from beg. Fasten off.

LEFT FRONT

Beg at lower edge with A, ch 31 (34, 37, 40).

Foundation (RS): Sc in second ch from hook and in each ch across—30 (33, 36, 39) sts. Ch 1, sc in each sc across.

Beg Plaid Pattern on Row 3 at point A and work to point B (C, D, E). Cont est pattern through completion of Row 26 (30, 34, 38). Fasten off A.

Center Border: Row 1: With B, sc in each sc across. **Row 2:** With WS facing, sl st in back lp of each sc across and fasten off.

Upper Body: With RS facing, join C in first rem lp of Border Row 2. Ch 1, sc in same lp as joining and in each rem lp across. Cont in sc for 17 (21, 25, 29) more rows.

Neck Shaping: With RS facing, sc in each sc across, leaving last 12 (14, 14, 16) sts unworked. Cont on rem 18 (19, 22, 23) sts for 7 rows more. Fasten off.

RIGHT FRONT

With A, ch 31 (34, 37, 40). Work Foundation as for Left Front. Fasten off A.

With WS facing, join C with sl st in first sc. Ch 1, sc in same sc as joining and in each sc across. Cont in C sc for 24 (28, 32, 36) rows more. Fasten off C.

With RS facing join B with sl st in first sc at right edge. Ch 1, sc in same sc as joining and in each sc across. Rep Center Border Row 2 as for Left Front.

Upper Body: With RS facing, join A in first rem lp of Border Row 2. Ch 1, sc in same lp as joining and in each rem lp across. Work another sc row with A.

Beg Plaid Pattern on Row 3 at point A and work to point B (C, D, E). Cont est pattern for 15 (19, 23, 27) rows more. Fasten off.

Neck Shaping: With RS facing sk first 12 (14, 14, 16) sts. Join correct color in Plaid Pattern with sl st in next sc. Ch 1, sc in same sc as joining; cont following est pattern across rem 17 (18, 21, 22) sts. In est pattern, work 7 rows more on rem 18 (19, 22, 23) sts. Fasten off.

SLEEVES (make two)

Beg at the lower edge with A, ch 25 (27, 29, 31). Sc in second ch from hook and in each ch across—24 (26, 28, 30) sts. Fasten off.

Beg Body Pattern on Row 1. Cont in pattern, inc 1 st each edge every other row 10 (10, 10, 12) times; then inc 1 st each edge every fourth row 2 (3, 4, 3) times. Cont in pattern on 48 (52, 56, 60) sts to 9 (10, 11½, 11½) in./22.9 (25.4, 29.2, 29.2)cm from beg. Fasten off.

FINISHING

Embroidery

Plaid: Thread tapestry needle with an 18-in./45.7cm double strand of D. Work cross-stitches to form plaid on lower Left Front and upper Right Front, following Plaid Pattern. See p. 51 for more information on working cross-stitch embroidery.

Right Front Scottie: Using a double strand of A. Beg working cross-stitches on fifth (ninth, eleventh, thirteenth) white row from lower edge on eleventh (thirteenth, fourteenth, sixteenth) st.

Left Front Scottie: Using a double strand of A, beg working cross-stitches on third white row and on eighth (ninth, eleventh, twelfth) st from right edge.

Sewing: Join shoulder seams. Place cardigan on flat surface, pin to measurements, cover with damp towel, and

leave to dry. Place markers 6 (6½, 7, 7½) in./15.2 (16.5, 17.8, 19.1)cm each side of shoulder seams. Set in sleeves between markers. Join underarm and side seams.

Body Band: With RS facing, join A with sl st in first rem ch of Foundation at left front edge. Ch 1, sc in same ch as joining. Working along opposite edge of Foundation ch, sc in each ch across lower edge. In right front corner, work 2 sc. Work 44 (52, 60, 68) sc evenly spaced to neck, 2 sc in first sc in corner, 22 (24, 24, 26) sc to

Sc in same sc as last neck st, 2 sc in side of neckband. Working in rem lps from Body Band Rnd 2, sc in each of next 46 (54, 62, 70) sc—49 (57, 65, 73) sts.

Row 2: Ch 1, sc in each of first 5 sc; * ch 2, sk 2 sc, sc in each of next 8 (10, 12, 14) sc; rep from * for 5 buttonholes, ending last rep sc in last 2 sc.

Row 3: Ch 1, sc in each sc across, working 2 sc in each ch-2 sp.

Lower Edge and Left Front Band: Sc in same sc as last st of right front band. With WS facing, sc in each rem lp along lower edge; 2 sc in corner, sc in each rem lp of left band, working 3 sc along side of neckband.

Row 2: Ch 1, sc in each of 49 (57, 65, 73) sts.

Row 3: Rep Row 2. Fasten off.

Embellishment: Sew buttons opposite buttonholes, using a French Knot, if desired: Thread tapestry needle with single strand of D; bring yarn from back to front and through one hole of button; wrap yarn around needle 4 times; then take yarn through second hole and to back of fabric; pull slowly to complete knot. Secure end of yarn to WS. Tie bow at neck of each Scottie.

shoulder, 20 (22, 22, 24) sc along back neck, 22 (24, 24, 26) sc to corner, 2 sc in corner, 44 (52, 60, 68) sc evenly spaced to lower edge, sc in same ch as first sc. Join with sl st in front lp of first sc. **Rnd 2:** Sl st in front lp of each sc around. At end, join with sl st in first sc and fasten off.

Neckband

With WS facing, join A with sl st in back lp of second corner sc of neck edge. Ch 1, working in rem lps, sc in same sc as joining and in each of next 9 (11, 11, 13) sc, sc2tog, sc in next sc, sc2tog. Sc in each of the next 36 (38, 38, 40) back lps, sc2tog, sc in next sc, sc2tog, sc in rem 10 (12, 12, 14) sc.

Row 2: Ch 1, sc in first 9 (11, 11, 13) sc, sc2tog, sc in next sc, sc2tog, sc in next 34 (36, 36, 38) sc, sc2tog, sc in next sc, sc2tog, sc in 9 (11, 11, 13) sc.

Row 3: Ch 1, sc in first 8 (10, 10, 12) sc, sc2tog, sc in next sc, sc2tog, sc in next 32 (34, 34, 36) sc, sc2tog, sc in next sc, sc2tog, sc in 8 (10, 10, 12) sc.

Tip for Success

As you embroider on the crocheted fabric, keep your stitching loose enough so that it lies flat and smooth.

English Schoolgirl Cape

● ● ● ● ● ● ● ● ● ● ● ● ● ● ● ● ● ● ● ●

Intermediate

Made from side to side in washable chenille using a unique bobble stitch, this cape can be worked up very quickly. Openings at the front allow your child to have access to her hands. The roomy hood will keep out the drafts on a cool day.

MATERIALS

● Lion Brand Chenille Sensations, 100% acrylic (worsted weight), 1.4-oz./40g skeins (each 87 yd./ 82m): 6 (8, 10) skeins Mulberry #142 (MC), 1 skein Brick #134 (CC)

● Size 8/H (5.00mm) aluminum crochet hook **or size needed to obtain gauge**

● Yarn needle

● JHB International Buttons, ⅞ in./2.2cm in diameter: 3 Equator #90348

GAUGE

● In Body Pattern: 10 sts = 3 in./7.6cm and 15 rows = 4 in./10.2cm (narrowest portion); 10 sts = 3 in./7.6cm and 9 rows = 4 in./10.2cm (widest portion)

SIZES

● For babies, 0–6 (7–12 , 13–18) months; directions are written for the smallest size with changes for the larger sizes in parentheses

FINISHED MEASUREMENTS

● At shoulders (buttoned): 22 (26¼, 30½) in./ 55.9 (66.6, 77.5)cm

● Length: 12¾ (14, 15¼) in./ 32.4 (35.6, 38.7)cm

67

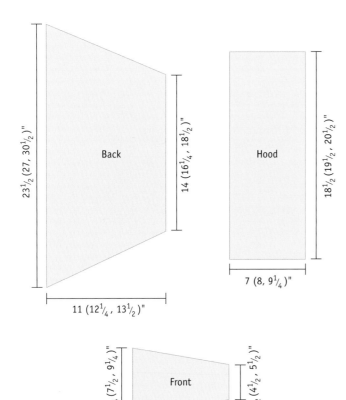

Back

23½ (27, 30½)"

14 (16¼, 18½)"

11 (12¼, 13½)"

Hood

18½ (19½, 20½)"

7 (8, 9¼)"

Front

5¾ (7½, 9¼)"

3½ (4½, 5½)"

ABBREVIATIONS

- sc2tog = draw up lp in each of next 2 sts, yo and draw through all 3 lps on hook

- hdc2tog = in each of next 2 sts (yo and draw up lp), yo and draw through all 5 lps on hook

● ● ● ● ● ● ● ● ● ● ●

Before You Begin

- The cape is worked from side to side in three separate pieces. The hood is worked separately.

- For a perfect fit, pay careful attention to the row gauge.

- Turn at the end of each row.

BACK

Beg at side edge with MC, ch 38 (42, 46).

Foundation: Sc in second ch from hook and in each ch across—37 (41, 45) sts.

Body Pattern: Row 1 (RS): Ch 1, sc in first sc; (ch 1, sk 1 sc, tr in next sc) across, ending ch 1, sk 1 sc, sc in last sc.

Row 2: Ch 1, sc in first sc; (sc in skipped sc two rows below, sc in tr) across, ending sc in skipped sc two rows below, sc in last sc.

Row 3: Ch 1, sc in first sc and each of the next 6 (7, 8) sc, hdc in each of the next 10 (11, 12) sc, dc in each of the next 10 (11, 12) sc, tr in last 10 (11, 12) sc.

Row 4: Ch 1, sc in each st across.

Rep Rows 1 to 4 for 12 (14, 16) times more. Fasten off.

FRONT (make two)

Work as for Back. Rep Body Pattern Rows 1 to 4 for 3 (4, 5) times total. Fasten off.

HOOD

With MC, ch 24 (28, 32). Work Foundation as for Back—23 (27, 31) sts.

Body Pattern Rows 1–2: Same as for Back.

Rows 3–4: Ch 1, sc in each sc across.

Rep Rows 1 to 4 for 16 (17, 18) times more. Fasten off.

FINISHING

Join back to fronts from neck down 4 in./10.2cm, skip next 5 in./12.7cm for arm opening, join rem 2 (3¼, 4½) in./5.1 (8.2, 11.4)cm.

Neckband: With RS facing, join MC at top corner with sl st. Ch 1, sc in same sp as joining. Working 1 st in each row across, sc in each of next 9 rows, working hdc2tog over next 2 rows, hdc in each row across to last 10, sc in each of last 10 rows—50 (58, 66) sts; turn. Ch 1, sc in

Row 4: With RS facing, join MC with sl st in lower right front corner. Ch 1, sc in same sc as joining. Sc in each sc and ch across to corner; sl st across top of band.

Row 5: With WS facing, sl st between first 2 sts; (sl st between next 2 sts) to corner; sl st in each sc along front; (sl st between next 2 sts) along lower edge; sl st in each sc along next front; sl st across top of front band.

Row 6: With RS facing, (sl st between next 2 sts) around, ending near hood on the opposite side. Fasten off.

Hood Trim: With RS facing, using CC, sl st in each st along hood edge. With WS facing, sl st between next 2 sts across. With RS facing, sl st between next 2 sts across and fasten off.

Tassel: Cut fifty 10-in/25.4cm long strands of CC and one extra piece. Smooth out strands and hold tog in a bundle. Fold in half to form lp. Using extra piece, tie tightly through lp. With another strand, wrap tassel several times approx ½ in./1.3cm from first tie and around entire bundle; tie tightly. Use ends of first tie to attach tassel to tip of hood. Trim ends.

Arm Opening Trim (make two): With RS facing, using CC, join in first st at top of opening. Sl st in each st around, ending join with sl st in first sl st.

Sew buttons opposite buttonholes.

each of first 6 sc, (sc2tog) 4 times, hdc2tog across to last 14 sts, (sc2tog) 4 times, sc in last 6 sc 45 (54, 61) sts. Fasten off.

Hood: RSs tog, fold hood in half to measure 9¼ (9¾, 10¼) in. Using MC, sl st edges tog along one side for back seam. With RSs tog, pin hood to neckband, placing hood seam at center of back neck. Easing in fullness, sl st hood to neck of cape.

Body Band

With RS facing, join MC with sl st in first sc at left front neck edge.

Row 1: Ch 1, sc in same sc as joining. Sc in each of next 35 (39, 43) sts, 2 sc in last sc. Working along lower edge, work 20 (24, 28) sc evenly to seam, hdc in seam, 66 (76, 86) sc evenly to next seam, hdc in seam, 20 (24, 28) sc evenly to corner; 2 sc in first sc of right front, sc in each rem sc across.

Row 2: Ch 1, sc in first sc, (ch 2, sk 2 sc, sc in each of the next 10 sc) 3 times; sc in each sc to corner; sl st in each sc along lower edge; sc in each sc along left front.

Row 3: Ch 1, sc in each sc along left front. Fasten off.

A Different Look

For a special holiday gift, make this cape in the appropriate colors: orange and black for Halloween, red and green for Christmas, blue and white for Chanukah, or red and white for Valentine's Day.

Wild, Wild West

Remember Dale Evans and Roy Rogers?
How about Davy Crockett? Revisit your favorite
old TV westerns when you work up the projects in this section.
You'll find all types of western-style sweaters
and a coonskin cap for a giggle.

Western Jacket

• •

Intermediate

A very soft, washable wool combined with a simple pattern stitch makes the body of this jacket pure pleasure to crochet. The shawl collar is easy to work. For fun, cut the back pockets off of an old pair of jeans and sew them onto the jacket; don't forget to add some fringe to the collar.

MATERIALS

- Knit One, Crochet Too! Crème Brulee, 100% wool (DK, Superwash), 1.75-oz./50g skeins (each 131 yd./120m): 5 (5, 6, 7, 8) skeins Seaport #659 (MC), 3 (3, 3, 4, 5) skeins Camel #893 (A), 3 (3, 3, 4, 5) skeins Fawn Heather #822 (B)

- Size 5/F (4.00mm) aluminum crochet hook **or size needed to obtain gauge**

- Tapestry needle

- Back pockets from blue jeans: 2

- Sewing needle

- Sewing thread: Gold

- JHB International Buttons: 3 (3, 4, 4, 4) Canoe Buttons #20071

GAUGE

- In Body Pattern: 19 sts = 4 in./ 10.2cm; 26 rows = 7 in./17.8cm

SIZES

- For children, 4 (6, 8, 10, 12); directions are written for the smallest size with changes for the larger sizes in parentheses

FINISHED MEASUREMENTS

- Chest (buttoned): 30 (33¼, 34¼, 36¾, 40¼) in./ 76.2 (84.4, 87, 92, 102.2)cm

- Length: 13 (15, 17, 19, 21) in./33 (38.1, 43.2, 48.3, 53.3)cm

ABBREVIATIONS

- dc2tog = (dc in next st until 2 lps rem on hook) twice, yo and draw through all 3 lps on hook

- sc2tog = draw up lp in each of next 2 sts, yo and draw through all 3 lps on hook

- rev sc = reverse single crochet: working from left to right (instead of from right to left), ch 1, sc in each sc

● ● ● ● ● ● ● ● ○ ○ ○ ○

Before You Begin

- Note that the border is added after the main body of the jacket has been crocheted.

- To change colors in double crochet: With the current color, work the double crochet until two loops remain on the hook; with the next color, yarn over and complete the double crochet.

- To change colors in single crochet: Draw up a loop with the current color; with the next color, complete the single crochet.

- To change colors at the end of a row: In the last stitch, draw up a loop with the current color; with the next color, complete the stitch.

- Carry the color not in use loosely along the side of the work.

- Turn at the end of each row.

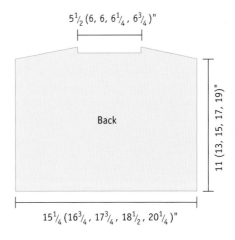

5½ (6, 6, 6¼, 6¾)"

Back

11 (13, 15, 17, 19)"

15¼ (16¾, 17¾, 18½, 20¼)"

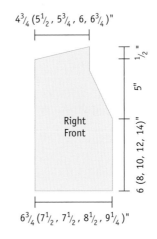

4¾ (5½, 5¾, 6, 6¾)"

½"

5"

Right Front

6 (8, 10, 12, 14)"

6¾ (7½, 7½, 8½, 9¼)"

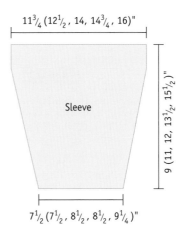

11¾ (12½, 14, 14¾, 16)"

Sleeve

9 (11, 12, 13½, 15½)"

7½ (7½, 8½, 8½, 9¼)"

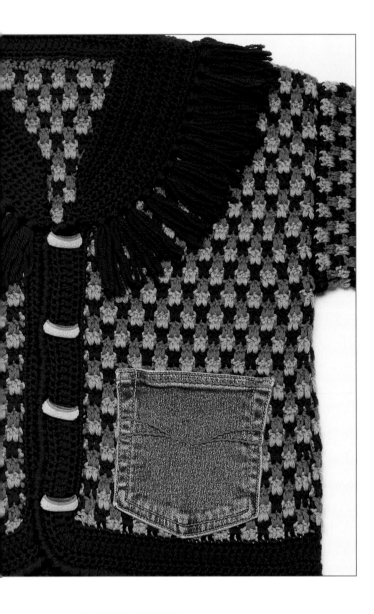

Row 3: With A, rep Row 1, changing to B in last st.

Row 4: With B, rep Row 2, changing to MC in last st.

Row 5: With MC, rep Row 1, changing to A in last st.

Row 6: With A, rep Row 2, changing to B in last st.

Rep Rows 1 to 6 for Body Pattern.

BACK

Beg at lower edge, with MC, ch 74 (82, 86, 90, 98).

Foundation (RS): Dc in fourth ch from hook, dc in next ch. * Ch 2, sk 2 ch, dc in each of next 2 ch; rep from * across, ending ch 2, sk 2 ch, dc in each of last 3 ch, changing to A in last st—72 (80, 84, 88, 96) sts; turn.

Row 2: With A, ch 1, sc in first dc; * ch 2, sk 2 dc, dc over ch-2 and into each of next 2 skipped ch; rep from * across, ending ch 2, sk 2 dc, sc in last dc and change to B.

Beg Body Pattern: Rep Rows 1 to 6 to approx 10½ (12½, 14½, 16½, 18½) in./26.7 (31.8, 36.9, 41.9, 47)cm from beg, ending with WS row.

Closing Row: With next color, ch 1, sc in sc; * sc in next 2 dc, dc over ch-2 sp and into next 2 skipped dc; rep from * across, ending sc in last 3 sts; turn.

Shoulder and Neck Shaping: With same color as last row, work **First Shoulder** as follows: Ch 1, sc in first 8 (9, 9, 10, 11) sts, hdc in next 8 (9, 9, 10, 11) sts, dc in next 7 (8, 10, 9, 10) sts. Fasten off.

With WS facing, work Second Shoulder as follows: Sk center 26 (28, 28, 30, 32) sts for neck. Join same color as last row with sl st in next st. Ch 3 (counts as dc), dc in each of next 6 (7, 9, 8, 9) sts, hdc in next 8 (9, 9, 10, 11) sts, sc in each rem st to end. Fasten off.

RIGHT FRONT

Beg at lower edge, with MC, ch 34 (38, 38, 42, 46). Work Foundation and Row 2 as for Back—32 (36, 36, 40, 44) sts; turn.

PATTERN STITCH
Body Pattern
multiple of 4 sts; rep of 6 rows

Row 1 (RS): With B, ch 1, sc in first sc; * dc over ch-2 and into each of 2 skipped dc **, ch 2, sk 2 dc; rep from * across, ending last rep at **, sc in last sc and change to MC; turn.

Row 2: With MC, ch 1, sc in first sc; * ch 2, sk 2 dc **, dc over ch-2 and into each of 2 skipped dc; rep from * across, ending last rep at **, sc in last sc and change to A; turn.

Beg Body Pattern: Rep Rows 1 to 6 to approx 6 (8, 10, 12, 14) in./15.2 (20.3, 25.4, 30.5, 35.6)cm from beg, ending with WS row.

V-Neck Shaping: Row 1 (RS): Keeping to est color pattern, ch 1, sc in sc, dc2tog; work as est to end; turn.

Row 2: Work est pattern across, ending 2 dc over ch-2 sp and into 2 skipped dc, ch 1, sk 1 dc, sc in last sc, changing to next color; turn.

Row 3: Ch 1, sc in sc, ch 2, sk 2 dc and cont pattern across; turn.

Row 4: Ch 1, work est pattern across, ending dc2tog, sc in sc; turn.

Cont dec as est until 23 (26, 28, 29, 32) sts rem.

Work to same length as Back, ending with RS row. Work Closing Row as for Back; turn. Work First Shoulder as for Back. Fasten off.

LEFT FRONT

Work as for Right Front, reversing neck and shoulder shaping.

SLEEVES (make two)

Beg at lower edge, with MC, ch 38 (38, 42, 42, 46). Work Foundation and Row 2 as for Back—36 (36, 40, 40, 44) sts.

Sleeve Shaping: Row 1: With next color, ch 1, 2 sc in first sc; cont pattern across, ending 2 sc in last sc and change to next color; turn.

Row 2: Ch 1, sc in sc, 2 sc in next sc; cont pattern across, ending 2 sc in next sc, sc in last sc and change to next color; turn.

Row 3: Ch 1, 2 sc in first sc, ch 2, sk 2 sc; cont pattern across, ending ch 2, sk 2 sc, 2 sc in last sc and change to next color.

Cont est inc pattern until there are 56 (60, 66, 70, 76) sts.

Work even to approx 9 (11, 12, 13½, 15½) in./ 22.9 (27.9, 30.5, 34.3, 39.4)cm from beg, ending with WS row. Rep Closing Row as for Back. Fasten off.

FINISHING

Join shoulder seams. Place markers 6½ (6¾, 7½, 8, 8½) in./16.5 (17.1, 19.1, 20.3, 21.6)cm each side of shoulder seams. Set in sleeves between markers. Join underarm and side seams.

Sleeve Edging: With RS facing, join MC at seam with sl st. Sc evenly around lower edge; join with sl st in first sc and fasten off. With WS facing, join double strand of MC with sl st in joining. Work 1 rnd of reverse sc, skipping every third sc. At end, join and fasten off.

Lower Body Band: With RS facing, join MC with sl st in first V-neck dec row on left front; work 23 (31, 39, 47, 55) sl sts more, evenly spaced, to lower edge. Fasten off. With RS facing, join MC with sl st in lower edge of right front and work 24 (32, 40, 48, 56) sl sts evenly spaced to V-neck; fasten off. With RS facing, join MC with sl st in first sl st on left front.

Row 1 (RS): Ch 1, sc in each sl st along front edge, 3 sc in first Foundation ch, sc in each ch across lower edge, working 3 sc in last ch, sc in each sl st on rem front; turn.

Row 2: Ch 1, sc in each sc around; turn.

Row 3: Ch 3 (counts as dc); dc in each sc around, working 3 dc in each corner; turn.

Row 4: Rep Row 2.

Row 5: Ch 1, sc in each sc around, working 3 sc in each corner; turn.

Row 6: Rep Row 2. Fasten off.

Neckband

With RS facing, beg just above right front band and using MC, work 21 sl sts to shoulder, work 29 (31, 31, 33, 35) sc evenly to next shoulder, work 21 sl sts to band; turn—71 (73, 73, 75, 77) sts.

Row 2: Ch 1, sc in 20 sl sts, sc2tog, sc across next 27 (29, 29, 31, 33) sc, sc2tog, sc in next 20 sl sts; turn.

Row 3: Ch 1, sc in 20 sc, sc2tog, sc in next 25 (27, 27, 29, 31) sc, sc2tog, sc in next 20 sc; turn—67 (69, 69, 71, 73) sts.

Row 4: Ch 3 (counts as dc); dc in each sc around; turn.

Row 5: Ch 1, sc in each st around; turn.

Row 6: Ch 1, sc in each sc around. At end, sc in first sc on band; turn to begin collar.

Collar

Row 1: Ch 1, sc in first 21 sc, (2 sc in next sc—inc made), sc in each of next 23 (25, 25, 27, 29) sc, inc, sc in next 20 sc, sc in first sc on band—69 (71, 71, 73, 75) sts; turn.

Row 2: Ch 1, sc in first sc, hdc in next 20 sc, inc, sc in next 25 (27, 27, 29, 31) sc, inc, hdc in next 20 sc, sc in next sc, sc in next sc on band—72 (74, 74, 76, 78) sts; turn.

Row 3: Ch 1, sc in 22 sts, inc, sc in next 25 (27, 27, 29, 31) sts, inc, sc in next 23 sts, sc in next sc on band—75 (77, 77, 79, 81) sts; turn.

Row 4: Ch 1, sc in first 4 sts, hdc in next 20 sts, inc, sc in next 27 (29, 29, 31, 33) sts, inc, hdc in 20 sts, sc in 2 sts, sc in next sc on band—78 (80, 80, 82, 84) sts; turn.

Row 5: Ch 1, sc in 23 sts, inc, sc in 29 (31, 31, 33, 35) sts, inc, sc in 24 sts, sc in next sc on band—81 (83, 83, 85, 87) sts; turn.

Row 6: Ch 1, sc in 5 sts, hdc in 20 sts, inc, sc in 31 (33, 33, 35, 37) sts, inc, hdc in 20 sts, sc in 3 sts, sc in next sc on band—84 (86, 86, 88, 90) sts; turn.

Row 7: Ch 1, sc in 24 sts, inc, sc in 33 (35, 35, 37, 39) sts, inc, sc in 25 sts, sc in next sc on band—87 (89, 89, 91, 93) sts; turn.

Row 8: Ch 1, sc in 6 sts, hdc in 20 sts, inc, sc in 35 (37, 37, 39, 41) sts, inc, hdc in 20 sts, sc in 4 sts, sc in next sc on band—90 (92, 92, 94, 96) sts; turn.

Row 9: Ch 1, sc in 25 sts, inc, sc in 37 (39, 39, 41, 43) sts, inc, sc in 26 sts, sc in next sc on band—93 (95, 95, 97, 99) sts; turn.

Row 10: Ch 1, sc in 7 sts, hdc in 20 sts, inc, sc in 39 (41, 41, 43, 45) sts, inc, hdc in 20 sts, sc in 5 sts, sc in next sc on band—96 (98, 98, 100, 102) sts; turn.

Row 11: Ch 1, sc in 26 sts, inc, sc in 41 (43, 43, 45, 47) sts, inc, sc in 27 sts, sc in next sc on band—99 (101, 101, 103, 105) sts; turn.

Row 12: Ch 1, sc in 8 sts, hdc in 20 sts, inc, sc in 43 (45, 45, 47, 49) sts, inc, hdc in 20 sts, sc in 6 sts, sc in next sc on band—102 (104, 104, 106, 108) sts; turn.

Row 13: Ch 1, sc in 27 sts, inc, sc in 45 (47, 47, 49, 51) sts, inc, sc in 28 sts, sc in next sc on band—105 (107, 107, 109, 111) sts; turn.

Row 14: Ch 1, sc in 9 sts, hdc in 20 sts, inc, sc in 47 (49, 49, 51, 53) sts, hdc in 20 sts, sc in 7 sts, sc in next sc on band. Fasten off.

Sew opening between collar sides and top of front bands using Mattress Stitch and MC.

Lower Body Edging: With RS facing, join double strand of MC in first rem sc near collar and on right front. Ch 1, work rev sc along front edge, skipping every sixth sc; on lower edge, sk every fourth sc, then sk every sixth sc again on rem side. Fasten off.

Fringe: Cut five 6-in./15.2cm strands of MC. Holding strands tog, fold in half to form lp. With WS of collar facing, take lp through third sc from collar edge; draw

ends through lp and pull up to form a knot. Make fringe for every other sc around collar, leaving last 2 sc at opposite edge free.

Pockets: Place jeans pockets onto jacket fronts with lowest portion of bottom next to lower band and with side edge about 1 in./2.5cm from front bands. Thread sewing needle with gold thread and sew around three sides, leaving top open.

Buttons: Place markers for 3 (3, 4, 4, 4) buttons with the first one at 1 in./2.5cm from top of rev sc front border and last one 1 in./2.5 cm from first corner sc row and the rem 1 (1, 2, 2, 2) evenly spaced between. Sew on buttons. For buttonholes, stretch sp between 2 dc to accommodate button.

Tip for Success

Because there was some decorative gold stitching remaining on the pockets I used, I decided to weave some Camel yarn through the machine stitches to highlight it. Next, I basted the pockets in position on the jacket. Since it can be difficult to sew through all the layers, I used my trusty thimble and a needle and gold thread, to blind-stitch the pocket edges in place.

Miner's Denim Pullover

● ●

Intermediate

A combination of cables and a luxurious soft cotton-blend yarn make this pullover very easy to wear. Notice the rolled turtleneck, once seen only in knitted garments.

MATERIALS

- Plymouth's Wildflower, 51% cotton/49% acrylic (DK weight), 1.75-oz./50g skeins (each 137 yd./ 125.2m): 8 (10, 12, 14) skeins Denim #10

- Size 5/F (4.00mm) aluminum crochet hook **or size needed to obtain gauge**

- Tapestry needle

GAUGE

- In Body Pattern: 22 sts and 25 rows = 5 in./12.7cm

SIZES

- For children, 2 (4, 6, 8); directions are written for the smallest size with changes for the larger sizes in parentheses

FINISHED MEASUREMENTS

- Chest: 28½ (32, 34, 37) in./ 72.4 (81.3, 86.4, 93.9)cm

- Length: 15 (16½, 18, 19½) in./ 38.1 (41.9, 45.7, 49.6)cm

ABBREVIATIONS

- fpdc = front post double crochet: yo, insert hook from front to back then to front to go around dc post, draw up lp, (yo and draw through 2 lps on hook) twice.

- fpdc over fpdc = on RS, fpdc over fpdc 2 rows below, skipping sc behind new st; on WS, sc in top of fpdc

- hdc2tog = in each of next 2 sts (yo and draw up lp), yo and draw through all 5 lps on hook

- hdc post = yo and draw up lp around post of next st, yo and draw through all 3 lps on hook

● ● ● ● ● ● ● ● ● ● ● ●

Before You Begin

- The cables on this sweater are made in a front post double crochet stitch.

- Turn at the end of each row.

BACK

Beg at lower edge, ch 65 (72, 77, 84).

Foundation: Row 1 (RS): Dc in fourth ch from hook and in each ch across—63 (70, 75, 82) sts.

Row 2: Ch 1, sc in each dc across.

Row 3: Ch 1, sc in each of first 3 (3, 2, 2) sc. * Fpdc over next dc from Row 1, sc in next sc, sk next dc, fpdc over each of next 4 dc from Row 1, sc in next sc, sk next dc. Rep from * across, ending fpdc over next dc from Row 1, sc in each of last 3 (3, 2, 2) sc.

Row 4: Ch 1, sc in each sc and fpdc across.

Row 5: Ch 1, sc in each of first 3 (3, 2, 2) sc. * Fpdc over next fpdc, sc in next sc, fpdc over each of next 4 fpdc, sc in sc. Rep from * across, ending fpdc over last fpdc, sc in each of last 3 (3, 2, 2) sc.

Row 6: Rep Row 4.

Rows 7–8: Rep Rows 4 to 5.

Row 9: Rep Row 4.

Body Pattern: Row 1 (RS): Ch 1, sc in each of first 3 (3, 2, 2) sc. *Fpdc over next fpdc, sc in next sc, (sk next 2 fpdc, fpdc in third fpdc, fpdc in fourth fpdc, fpdc in first fpdc, fpdc in second fpdc—cable made), sc in next sc. Rep from * across, ending fpdc over last fpdc, sc in each of last 3 (3, 2, 2) sc.

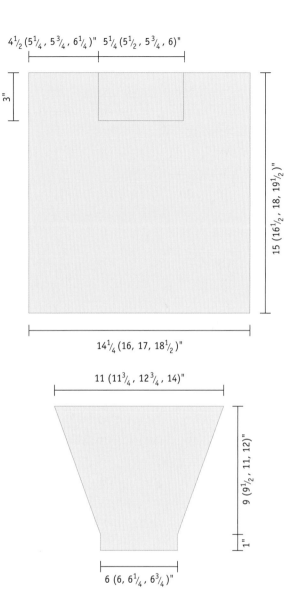

Row 2: Ch 1, sc in each sc and fpdc across.

Row 3: Ch 1, sc in each of first 3 (3, 2, 2) sc. * Fpdc over next fpdc, sc in next sc, fpdc over each of next 4 fpdc, sc in sc. Rep from * across, ending fpdc over last fpdc, sc in each of last 3 (3, 2, 2) sc.

Row 4: Rep Row 2.

Rep Rows 1 to 4 to approx 15 (16½, 18, 19½) in./ 38.1 (41.9, 45.7, 49.9)cm from beg, ending with RS row. Fasten off.

FRONT

Work as for Back to approx 12 (13½, 15, 16½) in./ 30.5 (34.3, 38.1, 41.9)cm from beg, ending with RS row.

Neck Shaping: Ch 1, sc in each of first 20 (23, 25, 28) sts; sk center 23 (24, 25, 26) sts; in next st join new strand (draw up lp, ch 1). Sc in same st as joining and in each of rem 19 (22, 24, 27) sts.

For size 2: End left neck edge fpdc in fpdc, sc in last 2 sc; beg right neck edge sc in first 2 sc, fpdc in fpdc.
For size 4: End left neck edge fpdc in next 2 fpdc, sc in last 2 sc; beg right neck edge sc in first 2 sc, fpdc in next 2 fpdc. **For size 6:** End left neck edge with fpdc over fpdc, sc in last sc; beg right neck edge with sc in first sc, fpdc over fpdc. **For size 8:** End left neck edge with fpdc over next 2 fpdc, sc in last sc; beg right neck edge with sc in first sc, fpdc over next 2 fpdc.

Working sides *separately and at the same time,* cont in pattern until piece measures same as Back. Fasten off.

SLEEVES (make two)

Beg at lower edge, ch 28 (28, 30, 32). Work Foundation Rows 1 and 2 as for Back—26 (26, 28, 30) sts.

Row 3: Ch 1, sc in 2 (2, 3, 4) sc. * Fpdc over next dc from Row 1, sc in next sc, sk next dc, fpdc over each of next 4 dc from Row 1, sc in next sc, sk next dc. Rep from * across, ending fpdc over next dc from Row 1, sc in last 2 (2, 3, 4) sc.

Row 4: Ch 1, sc in each sc and fpdc across.

Row 5: Ch 1, sc in first 2 (2, 3, 4) sc. * Fpdc over next fpdc, sc in next sc, fpdc over each of next 4 fpdc, sc in sc. Rep from * across, ending fpdc over last fpdc, sc in 2 (2, 3, 4) sc.

Rep Rows 4 to 5 for pattern, inc 1 st each edge on next row—28 (28, 30, 32) sts. Working new sts in sc, cont in est pattern inc 1 st each edge every second row 3 (3, 4, 6) times more; then inc 1 st each edge every fourth row for 7 (9, 9, 9) times. Cont in pattern on 48 (52, 56, 62) sts to approx 10 (10½, 12, 13) in./25.4 (26.7, 30.5, 33)cm from beg, ending with RS row. Fasten off.

FINISHING

Join shoulder seams. Place markers on each side edge 5½ (6, 6½, 7) in./14 (15.2, 16.5, 17.8)cm from shoulder seam. Set in sleeves between markers. Join underarm and side seams.

With RS facing, join yarn with sl st close to one lower side seam. Working along opposite lps of Foundation, sl st in each ch around. Fasten off.

Neckband
With RS facing, join yarn with sl st near right shoulder seam. Ch 1, work 27 (28, 29, 30) sc evenly spaced along back neck. Work 13 sc evenly spaced along side of neck, ending before shaping. Hdc2tog over side of neck and front neck. Work 21 (22, 23, 24) sc evenly spaced along neck, hdc2tog over neck and side, then work 13 sc evenly spaced to shoulder. Join with sl st in front lp of first sc.

Size It Right!

Before beginning any project, pay attention to the gauge given in the instructions. Be sure to make a test swatch in the stitch listed and then measure your gauge carefully. This way you can be sure that the dimensions of your finished garment will match those of the pattern. Experiment with smaller or larger hooks until you get the correct gauge.

Rnd 2: Sl st in front lp of each sc around. Fasten off.

Rnd 3: Join yarn with sl st in first rem back lp. Ch 1, hdc in same sc as join and in each rem lp around. Join with sl st in first hdc.

Rnd 4: Ch 1, sc in same hdc as joining. * Hdc post over next hdc, sc in next hdc; rep from * around. At end, join with sl st in front lp of first sc.

Rnd 5: Sl st in front lp of each st around.

Rnd 6: Sc in each rem back lp around.

Rnds 7–10: Sc in each sc around. After Rnd 10, fasten off. Let neckband form a natural roll.

Buffalo-Plaid Jacket

●●●●●●●●●●●●●●●●●●●●●●●●●●●●●●

Made in the style of the popular
baseball jackets that boys enjoy,
this top is stitched in single crochet
in a two-color pattern stitch.
The zipper closure is great
for children and very easy
to attach.

Experienced

MATERIALS

- Lion Brand Wool-Ease, 80% acrylic/20% wool
  (machine-washable, worsted weight), 3-oz./85g skeins
  (each 197 yd./185.3m): 3 (4, 4, 5, 6) skeins Loden
  #177 (MC) and 2 (2, 2, 3, 3) skeins Cranberry
  #138 (CC)

- Size 6/G (4.25mm) aluminum crochet hook
  or size needed to obtain gauge

- Size 5/F (4.00mm) aluminum crochet hook

- Separating zipper: 14 (16, 18, 20, 22) in./
  35.6 (40.6, 45.7, 50.8, 55.9)cm long

- Tapestry needle

- Sewing needle

- Matching sewing thread

GAUGE

- In sc and color pattern: 25 sts
  and 30 rows = 6 in./15.2cm

- In solid sc: 16 sts and
  16 rows = 4 in./10.2cm

SIZES

- For children, 4 (6, 8, 10, 12);
  directions are written for the
  smallest size with changes for
  the larger sizes in parentheses

FINISHED MEASUREMENTS

- Chest (zipped): 28¾ (30½, 32½, 34½, 36½) in./ 73 (77.5, 82.6, 87.7, 92.7)cm

- Length: 16 (18, 20, 22, 24) in./40.6 (45.7, 50.8, 55.9, 61)cm

ABBREVIATIONS

- sc2tog = draw up lp in each of next 2 sts, yo and draw through all 3 lps on hook

Before You Begin

- The Plaid Pattern is worked from charts. Read from right to left for right side rows and from left to right for wrong side rows.

- While working the Plaid Pattern, carry the color not in use loosely along the top of the last row, and work over it as you go.

- To change colors in single crochet: Draw up a loop with the current color; with the next color, complete the single crochet.

- Turn at the end of each row.

Tip for Success

Demystify the two-color process used for the Buffalo-Plaid Pattern by making a small practice swatch as follows:

With MC, ch 16 sts. Sc in second ch and in each ch across—15 sts. For first RS row, sc with MC in first 4 sc. Keeping unused strand along WS, (draw up MC lp in next sc, and with CC complete the sc; then with CC draw up lp in next sc, complete sc with MC) twice. Draw up CC lp in next sc, and with MC complete the sc. Work 5 sc with MC and turn. For WS row, ch 1, sc in first 4 sc with MC. With MC, draw up lp in next sc, and with CC complete the sc. Keeping strand not in use on WS, cont as est across next 4 sts; then with MC, complete row.

On the jacket you will carry the unused color across the solid blocks, working over it as you go.

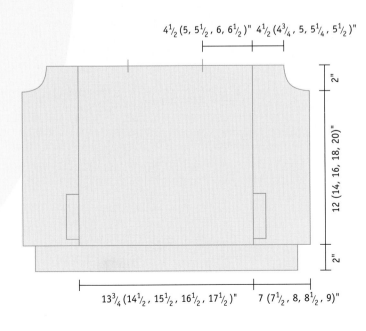

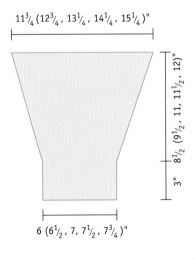

BUFFALO-PLAID PATTERN

Left Front

Back

Key

● Loden (MC)

● Cranberry (CC)

Right Front

BACK

Lower Ribbing: Working from side to side, with smaller hook and MC, ch 10.

Foundation: Sc in second ch from hook and in each ch across—9 sts; turn.

Row 2: Ch 1, working in back lps, sc in each sc across; turn.

Rep Row 2 for 113 (121, 129, 137, 145) more rows; *do not turn at end of last row.* Working across one long edge, ch 1, sc in each row across as follows: Work 29 (31, 33, 35, 37) sc for right front and fasten off. Work 57 (61, 65, 69, 73) sc for back and fasten off. Work 29 (31, 33, 35, 37) sc for left front and fasten off— 115 (123, 131, 139, 147) total sts.

Body: With RS facing and larger hook, join CC with sl st in first sc on back. Ch 1, beg Row 1 of Back Buffalo Plaid Pattern chart at size you are making and work to B. Rep A to B across, ending by working from C to your size. Follow chart through completion of Row 8; then rep Rows 1 to 8 for Buffalo Plaid Pattern until piece measures approx 16 (18, 20, 22, 24) in./40.6 (45.7, 50.8, 55.9, 61)cm from beg, ending with WS row. Fasten off.

LEFT FRONT

With RS facing and larger hook, join CC (CC, CC, MC, MC) with sl st in first left front sc. Ch 1, beg Row 1 of Left Front Buffalo-Plaid Pattern chart at your size and work to B. Rep A to B across, ending with working from C to your size. Work Rows 2 to 3 from chart.

Pocket Opening: Row 4 (WS): Cont est pattern across, leaving last 4 sts unworked.

Work Rows 5 to 8 from chart; then rep Rows 1 to 8 for Buffalo-Plaid Pattern on 25 (27, 29, 31, 33) sts until pocket opening measures approx 4 in./10.2cm, from beg, ending with WS row. Piece should measure approx 7 in./ 17.8cm from beg.

At beg of next row, ch 5. With correct colors according to chart, sc in second ch from hook and in each of next 3 ch. Cont in Buffalo-Plaid Pattern on 29 (31, 33, 35, 37) sts until piece measures approx 14 (16, 18, 20, 22) in./35.6 (40.6, 45.7, 50.8, 55.9)cm from beg, ending with WS row.

Neck Shaping: Work est pattern across, leaving last 7 (8, 9, 10, 11) sts unworked. Cont in pattern, skipping 1 st at neck edge every row 3 times. Work even on rem 19 (20, 21, 22, 23) sts to approx 16 (18, 20, 22, 24) in./40.6 (45.7, 50.8, 55.9, 61)cm from beg, ending with WS row. Fasten off.

RIGHT FRONT

With RS facing and larger hook, join CC with sl st in first right front sc. Ch 1, beg Row 1 of Right Front Buffalo-Plaid Pattern chart at your size and work to B. Rep A to B, ending last rep by working from C to your size.

Reversing pocket opening and neck shaping, work as for Left Front.

POCKET LININGS (make two)

Using larger hook and MC, ch 19. Work in sc on the 18 sts until piece measures approx 5 in./12.7cm from beg. Fasten off.

SLEEVES (make two)

Cuff: With MC and smaller hook, ch 14. Work as for Lower Ribbing for 27 (29, 31, 33, 35) total rows; *do not turn.* Ch 1, working 1 st per row, sc evenly across top of ribbing—27 (29, 31, 33, 35) sts. Change to larger hook. Ch 1, sc in each sc across; turn. Cont in sc, inc 1 st each edge every other row 5 (6, 3, 4, 4) times; then every fourth row 5 (5, 8, 8, 9) times.

Work even on 47 (51, 53, 57, 61) sts until piece measures approx 11½ (12½, 14, 14½, 15) in./29.11 (31.8, 35.6, 36.9, 38.1)cm from beg, ending with WS row. Fasten off.

FINISHING

Join shoulder seams. Place markers 6¼ (6¾, 7, 7½, 8) in./15.8 (17.1, 17.8, 19.1, 20.3)cm each side of shoulder seams. Set in sleeves between markers.

Pocket Trim (make two): With RS facing and smaller hook, join MC with sl st in lower edge of pocket opening. Ch 1, work 16 sc evenly spaced across; turn. Sl st in back lp of each sc across; turn. Ch 1, sc in each rem lp across; turn. Work two more sc rows and fasten off. Sew trim edges to fronts.

With WS facing, place pocket lining onto front so that the top edge is next to front side edge and the lower side edge is next to ribbing. Leaving the edge near side free, sew in place.

Join underarm and side seams, joining pocket lining to back to complete side seam.

Right Front Band: With RS facing, using smaller hook, join MC with sl st in lower edge of ribbing. Ch 1, work 59 (67, 75, 83, 91) sc evenly spaced to neck; fasten off.

Left Front Band: With RS facing and smaller hook, join MC with sl st in front neck edge. Ch 1, work 59 (67, 75, 83, 91) sc evenly spaced to lower edge of ribbing; fasten off.

Collar

First Side: With MC and smaller hook, ch 4. Sc in second ch from hook and in next 2 ch—3 sts.

Row 1: Ch 1, sc in back lp of each sc across; turn.

Rows 2–3: Rep Row 1.

fasten off. Sew collar to inside of neck and along the ridge made by the first sl st row of the neckband.

Edging: With RS facing and smaller hook, join MC with a sl st in first sc in lower edge of right front band. Ch 1, sl st in each sc across, sl st in neckband and side of collar, sl st in every other row across collar, sl st in side of collar and neckband, sl st in each sc along left front. Fasten off.

Zipper: Baste closed zipper in place, matching top of teeth to top of neckband. With matching sewing thread, back-stitch in place.

Row 4: Ch 1, working in back lps, 2 sc in first sc for inc, sc in each sc across—4 sts; turn.

Rows 5–7: Rep Row 1.

Rows 8–11: Rep Rows 4 to 7—5 sts.

Row 12: Rep Row 4—6 sts.

Cont working sc in back lp for 27 (31, 35, 39, 43) more rows.

Second Side: Row 1: Ch 1, working in back lps, sc2tog, sc in each rem sc across—5 sts; turn.

Rows 2–4: Ch 1, sc in back lp of each sc across; turn.

Rows 5–8: Rep Rows 1 to 4—4 sts.

Rows 9–12: Rep Rows 1 to 4—3 sts. Fasten off after Row 12.

Neckband: With RS facing, using smaller hook and MC, work 59 (63, 67, 71, 75) sl sts evenly around neck. Fasten off. With RS facing, join MC with sl st in first st sl, ch 1, sc in same sl st as joining and in each rem sl st around neck; turn. Sl st in each sc around and

BUFFALO-PLAID JACKET   87

Pony Pullover

●●●●●●●●●●●●●●●●●●●●●●●●●

A couple of intarsia-style ponies leap over a garden on this cotton sweater. The button closure along the back makes for easy off and on.

Experienced

MATERIALS
- Plymouth Wildflower, 51% cotton/49% acrylic (DK weight), 1.75-oz./50g skeins (each 137 yd./125.2m): 6 (7, 9, 10) skeins Purple #45 (MC), 2 skeins Red #12 (A), 1 skein Rust #69 (B), 1 skein Turquoise #55 (C)
- Size 4/E (3.50mm) aluminum crochet hook **or size needed to obtain gauge**
- Tapestry needle
- JHB International Buttons, ⅝ in./1.6cm in diameter: 5 Buckskin #81060

GAUGE
- In Body Pattern: 18 sts and 15 rows = 4 in./10.2cm

SIZES
- For girls, (4, 6, 8, 10); directions are written for the smallest size with changes for the larger sizes in parentheses

FINISHED MEASUREMENTS
- Chest: 28 (30, 32, 34) in./71.1 (76.2, 81.3, 86.4)cm
- Length: 15½ (16½, 17½, 18½) in./39.4 (41.9, 44.5, 46)cm

ABBREVIATION
- sc2tog = draw up lp in each of next 2 sts, yo and draw through all 3 lps on hook

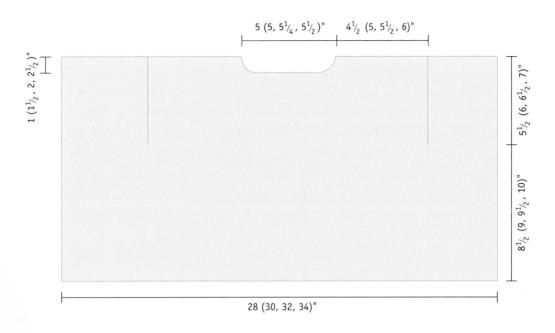

5 (5, 5¼, 5½)"   4½ (5, 5½, 6)"

1 (1½, 2, 2½)"

5½ (6, 6½, 7)"

8½ (9, 9½, 10)"

28 (30, 32, 34)"

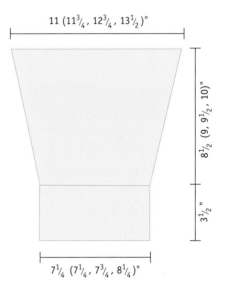

11 (11¾, 12¾, 13½)"

8½ (9, 9½, 10)"

3½"

7¼ (7¼, 7¾, 8¼)"

● ● ● ● ● ● ● ● ● ● ●
Before You Begin

- This pullover is worked in one piece to the armholes. The ponies, crocheted in the Body Pattern, are worked by following a chart. Read from right to left for the right side rows and from left to right for the wrong side rows. Use separate strands of yarn for each color section.

- Note that the cuff is made after the arm of the sleeve has been completed.

- To change colors in single crochet: Draw up a loop with the current color; with the next color, complete the single crochet.

- To change colors in double crochet: With the current color, work the double crochet until two loops remain on the hook; with the next color, yarn over and complete the double crochet.

- On each row, chain 1 at the beginning and turn at the end.

PONY PATTERN

Key
- ■ Rust
- ■ Red
- ■ Purple

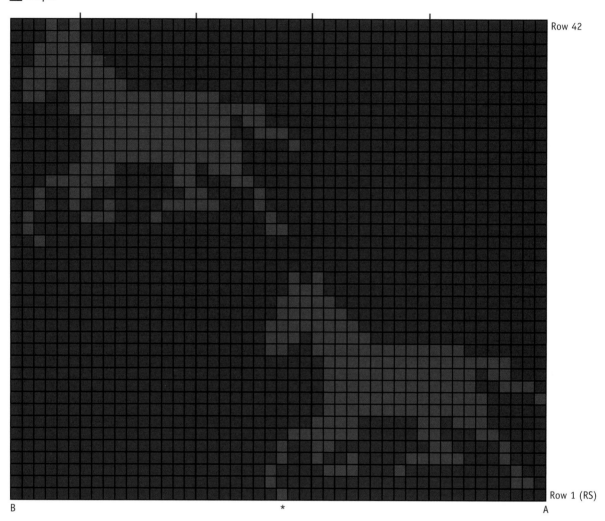

Row 42

Row 1 (RS)

B   *   A

PATTERN STITCH

Body Pattern

Row 1 (RS): Ch 1, hdc in first sc and each sc across; turn.

Row 2: Ch 1, sc in each hdc across; turn.

BODY

Beg at lower edge with MC, ch 127 (136, 145, 154). Hdc in second ch from hook and in each ch across—126 (135, 144, 153) sts. Sc in each hdc across. Work Body Pattern for 4 (6, 8, 10) rows. With MC, hdc in first 38 (44, 50, 54) sts; beg Pony Pattern chart at *, working pony with B, hdc to end of row. Working second pony with A, cont in Body Pattern through completion of Pony Pattern chart; work with MC for rem of pullover. *At the same time,* when piece measures approx 8½ (9, 9½, 10) in./21.7 (22.9, 24.1, 25.4)cm from beg, end with WS row. Work est pattern across first 31 (33, 35, 37) sts for left back; fasten off.

FRONT

With RS facing, join MC with sl st in next sc. Ch 1, hdc in same sc as joining. Cont pattern across next 63 (68, 73, 78) sts; turn. Leave rem sts to work later for right back. Work even on 64 (69, 74, 79) sts to approx 13 (13½, 14, 14½) in./33 (34.3, 35.6, 36.9)cm from beg, ending with RS row.

Neck Shaping: Ch 1, sc in first 22 (24, 26, 28) sts; turn. Ch 1, sk 1 sc, hdc in next 21 (23, 25, 27) sc; turn. Ch 1, sc in 21 (23, 25, 27) hdc. Work even to 14 (15, 16, 17) in./35.6 (38.1, 40.6, 43.2)cm from beg, ending with a sc row. Fasten off.

With WS facing, sk center 20 (21, 22, 23) sts; join MC with sl st in next st. Ch 1, sc in same st as joining and in each of next 21 (23, 25, 27) sts. Ch 1, hdc across to last 2 sts, sk 1 st, hdc in last st. Complete as for first side.

LEFT BACK

With WS facing, join MC with sl st in first hdc closest to front. Beg with sc row, work in pattern to same length as Front. Fasten off.

RIGHT BACK

With RS facing, join MC with sl st in first sc closest to front. Beg with hdc row, work in pattern to same length as front and fasten off.

SLEEVES (make two)

Beg at lower edge, with MC, ch 34 (34, 36, 38). Hdc in second ch from hook and in each ch across—33 (33, 35, 37) sts. Ch 1, 2 sc in first st, sc in each st across, ending 2 sc in last st.

Cont in Body Pattern, inc 1 st each edge every other row 1 (4, 5, 6) times more, then every fourth row 6 (5, 5, 5) times. Work even on 49 (53, 57, 61) sts to approx 8½ (9, 9½, 10) in./21.6 (22.9, 24.1, 25.4)cm from beg. Fasten off.

FINISHING

Pin garment pieces to measurements, cover with a damp cloth, and leave to dry.

Join shoulder and sleeve seams. Set in sleeves.

Cuff: With RS facing, join B with sl st near seam. Ch 1, work 33 (33, 35, 37) sc around. Work in rnds of sc until cuff measures 3½ in./8.9cm from beg. Turn cuff back. Sl st in each sc to center of sleeve, ch 6, sk 6 sts, sl st in each rem sc around and fasten off.

A Different Look

Want to make this pullover for a boy? Simply crochet the sweater in brown and the ponies in black. Then leave off the trims at the lower edges.

Flower: With RS facing, join C with sl st in first skipped sc and over ch. Ch 4, 10 dc in fourth ch from hook, sc in next ch and change to A. Sc in next sc, ch 8, 5 dc in fourth ch from hook, 5 dc in each rem ch, sc in next sc and change to C. Sc in next sc, ch 4, 10 dc in fourth ch from hook, sc in next ch and fasten off.

Neckband: With RS facing, join MC with sl st in top of left neck edge. Ch 1, work 53 (57, 61, 65) sc evenly spaced around neck; turn. **Row 2:** Ch 1, sc in back lp of each sc around; turn. Rep Row 2 to approx 2 in./5.1cm from beg, ending with RS row. Fasten off.

Lower Edging: With RS facing, join B with sl st in lower right back corner. Ch 1, work 126 (134, 146, 154) sc evenly spaced across; turn. Ch 1, sc in each sc across.

Flowers: With RS facing, join C with sl st in first sc at right edge, sc in same sc as joining. * Ch 4, 10 dc in fourth ch from hook, sc in next sc, changing to A; with A, sc in next sc, ch 8, 5 dc in fourth ch from hook and in

each rem ch, sc in next sc ** and change to C; with C, sc in next sc; rep from * across, ending last rep at **. Fasten off.

Back Neck

Leaving top 7 in./17.8cm free, join back seam. With RS facing, join MC with sl st in top corner of right neckband. Ch 1, work 13 sc along neckband, 36 sc evenly spaced around opening, 13 sc along neckband— 62 sts; turn.

Row 2: Ch 1, sc in 30 sc, sc2tog, sc in 4 sc, (ch 2, sk 2 sc, sc in next 2 sc) 5 times, sc in 6 sc; turn.

Row 3: Ch 1, sc in 8 sc, (2 sc in ch-2 sp, sc in 2 sc), sc in 2 sc, sc2tog, sc in each rem sc. Fasten off.

Sew buttons opposite buttonholes.

Daniel Boone Jacket

●●●●●●●●●●●●●●●●●●●●●●●●●●●●●●

Beginner

Trim this jacket with a leather-like
washable edging, add horse buttons
and a coonskin cap to help
a small boy look like
a mountain man.

MATERIALS

Jacket

- Elmore-Pisgah's Honeysuckle Yarns, 100% rayon
  chenille (machine-washable, sport weight), 1.5-oz./43g
  balls (each 88 yd./80m): 6 (8, 9, 10) balls Fudge #25

- Size 5/F (4.00mm) aluminum crochet hook
  or size needed to obtain gauge

- Needles: tapestry and sewing

- JHB International Buttons, 1⅛ in./2.8cm:
  3 Secretariat #20932

- Fringed suede trim: 2½ (3, 3, 3½) yd./
  2.3 (2.7, 2.7, 3.2)m

- Matching sewing thread

Cap

- Berroco's Furz, 50% nylon/
  25% wool/25% acrylic (bulky
  weight), 1.75-oz./50g balls
  (each 90 yd./82m):
  3 balls Taupe #3803 (A),
  1 ball Jungle Brown
  #3830 (B)

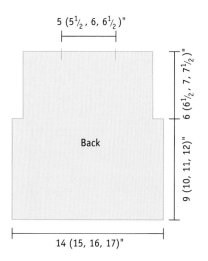

5 (5½, 6, 6½)"

6 (6½, 7, 7½)"

Back

9 (10, 11, 12)"

14 (15, 16, 17)"

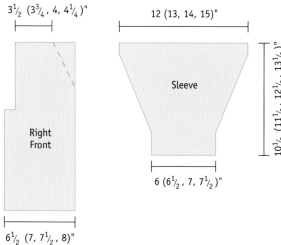

3½ (3¾, 4, 4¼)"

12 (13, 14, 15)"

Sleeve

10½ (11½, 12½, 13½)"

Right Front

6 (6½, 7, 7½)"

6½ (7, 7½, 8)"

- Size 8/H (5.00mm) aluminum crochet hook **or size needed to obtain gauge**
- Size 6/G (4.25mm) aluminum crochet hook

GAUGE
Jacket
- In sc: 11 sts = 3 in./7.6cm; 16 rows = 4 in./10.2cm

Cap
- In rnds of sc: 16 sts and 16 rnds = 4 in./10.2cm

SIZES
Jacket
- For children, 2(4, 6, 8); directions are written for the smallest size with changes for the larger sizes in parentheses

Cap
- One size

FINISHED MEASUREMENTS
Jacket
- Chest (buttoned): 28 (30, 32, 34) in./71.1 (76.2, 81.3, 86.4)cm
- Length: 15 (16½, 18, 19½) in./38.1 (41.9, 45.7, 49.6)cm

Cap
- Circumference: approx 25 in./63.5cm

ABBREVIATION
- sc2tog = draw up lp in each of next 2 sts, yo and draw through all 3 lps on hook

Before You Begin
- To change colors in single crochet: Draw up a loop with the current color; with the next color, complete the single crochet.
- When making the tail for the cap, carry the unused yarn loosely along the inside of the tail.
- Turn at the end of each row.

• Jacket •
BACK

Beg at lower edge, ch 53 (57, 60, 64). Sc in second ch from hook and in each ch across—52 (56, 59, 63) sts.

Body Pattern: Row 1 (WS): Ch 1, sc in each sc across; turn.

Row 2: Rep Row 1.

Cont in sc until work measures approx 9 (10, 11, 12) in./ 22.9 (25.4, 27.9, 30.5)cm from beg, ending with WS row. Fasten off.

Armhole Shaping: With RS facing, sk first 4 sts; join yarn with sl st in next st. Ch 1, sc in same sc as joining.

Sc in each of next 43 (47, 50, 54) sc, leaving last 4 sts unworked. Working on 44 (48, 51, 55) sts, cont in sc until piece measures approx 15 (16½, 18, 19½) in./ 38.1 (41.9, 45.7, 49.6)cm from beg. Fasten off.

RIGHT FRONT

Beg at lower edge, ch 25 (27, 29, 31). Sc in second ch from hook and in each ch across—24 (26, 28, 30) sc. Cont in sc to approx 8½ (9½, 10½, 11½) in./21.6 (24.1, 26.7, 29.1)cm from beg, ending with WS row.

Fringe Preparation: Step 1: Sc in back lp of each sc across. Working through both lps as usual, cont in sc to approx 9 (10, 11, 12) in./22.9 (25.4, 27.9, 30.5)cm from beg, ending with WS row.

Armhole Shaping: Sc in each sc across, leaving last 4 sts unworked—20 (22, 24, 26) sts.

Work even to same length as Back. Fasten off.

Fringe Preparation: Step 2: Holding front upside down and with RS facing, join yarn with sl st in first rem front lp.

Row 1 (RS): Ch 1, sc in same lp as joining and in each lp across—24 (26, 28, 30) sc.

Row 2: Ch 1, sc in each sc across.

Row 3: Ch 1, sc in first sc, sk next sc, sc in each of next 5 (6, 7, 8) sc, 3 sc in next sc, (sc in next 2 sc, sk next sc) twice, sc in next 2 sc, 3 sc in next sc, sc in each of next 5 (6, 7, 8) sc, sk next sc, sc in last sc.

Row 4: Rep Row 3. Fasten off.

LEFT FRONT

Work as for Right Front, reversing armhole shaping.

SLEEVES (make two)

Beg at lower edge, ch 23 (25, 26, 28). Sc in second ch from hook and in each ch across—22 (24, 25, 27) sts. Work in sc for 1½ in./3.8cm. Inc 1 st each edge every third row until there are 44 (48, 51, 55) sts. Cont in sc to approx 10½ (11½, 12½, 13½) in./26.7 (29.1, 31.8, 34.3)cm from beg. Fasten off.

FINISHING

Leaving 7 (8, 9, 10) sts at neck edge of each front free, join shoulder seams. Set in sleeves, joining sides to free armhole sts for square armholes. Join underarm and side seams.

Left Front Band: Place marker 11 (12½, 14, 15½) in./ 27.9 (31.8, 35.6, 39.4)cm from lower edge of front. With *WS* facing, join yarn with sl st in lower corner. Ch 1, sc in same sp as joining. Work 42 (48, 54, 60) sc evenly spaced to marker; turn. Ch 1, sc in each of first 2 sc; * ch 2, sk 2 sc, sc in each of next 10 sc; rep from * for three button-holes, working sc to end; turn. Ch 1, sc in each sc across to marker, working 2 sc in each ch-2 sp. Fasten off.

Right Front Band: Place a marker 11 (12½, 14, 15½) in./ 27.9 (31.8, 35.6, 39.4)cm from lower edge of front. With RS facing, join yarn with sl st in lower corner. Ch 1, work 43 (39, 55, 61) sc evenly spaced to marker; turn. Work 2 more sc rows and fasten off.

Sew buttons opposite buttonholes.

Trim: With RS facing, join yarn with sl st in center of back neck. Sl st evenly around entire body. At end, join with sl st in first sl st and fasten off. Turn back lapels and tack in place.

Fringe: Beg on left front, sew fringe onto scallops, across back, and then onto scallops of right front. Sew fringe along each sleeve seam at underarm and around each armhole.

• Coonskin Cap •

CAP

This cap is worked in continuous rnds. Do not join or ch 1 at the end of rnds.

Beg at crown with larger hook and A, ch 2; 6 sc in sec-ond ch from hook.

Rnd 1: 2 sc in each sc around—12 sts.

Rnd 2: (Sc in next sc, 2 sc in next sc) around—18 sts.

Rnd 3: (Sc in next 2 sc, 2 sc in next sc) around—24 sts.

Rnd 4: (Sc in next 3 sc, 2 sc in next sc) around—30 sts.

Rnd 5: (Sc in next 4 sc, 2 sc in next sc) around—36 sts.

Rnd 6: (Sc in next 5 sc, 2 sc in next sc) around—42 sts.

Rnd 7: (Sc in next 6 sc, 2 sc in next sc) around—48 sts.

Rnd 8: (Sc in next 7 sc, 2 sc in next sc) around—54 sts.

Rnd 9: (Sc in next 8 sc, 2 sc in next sc) around—60 sts.

Rnd 10: (Sc in next 9 sc, 2 sc in next sc) around—66 sts.

Rnd 11: (Sc in next 10 sc, 2 sc in next sc) around—72 sts.

Change to smaller hook.

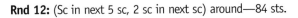

Rnd 12: (Sc in next 5 sc, 2 sc in next sc) around—84 sts.

Rnds 13–28: Sc in each sc around.

Rnd 29: (Sc in next 5 sc, 2 sc in next sc) around—98 sts.

Rnds 30–40: Sc in each sc around.

Rnd 41: (Sc in next 2 sc, sc2tog) around, ending sc in last 2 sc—74 sts.

Rnds 42–49: Sc in each sc around.

Rnd 50: Sl st in each sc around and fasten off.

For cuff: Make tight first roll with fuzzy side of roll out so that crown will be smoother side. Fold or roll again tightly. Fold once more so cuff measures approx 3 in./7.6cm deep.

TAIL

Using smaller hook and B, ch 2.

Rnd 1: 6 sc in second ch from hook.

Rnd 2: 2 sc in each sc around—12 sts.

Rnds 3–4: Sc in each sc around. In last st of Rnd 4, change to A.

Rnd 5: (2 sc in next sc, sc in next 5 sc) twice—14 sts.

Rnd 6: Sc in each sc around, changing to B in last st.

Rnd 7: (2 sc in next sc, sc in next 6 sc) twice—16 sts.

Rnds 8–9: Sc in each sc around, changing to A in last st of Rnd 9.

Tip for Success

Rolling the cuff of the coonskin cap is easy but tricky; you may need to try this a couple of times. Once the cuff looks like a western-style hat instead of a stocking cap, use the main color to tack it in place through all layers at several locations.

Rnd 10: (2 sc in next sc, sc in next 7 sc) twice—18 sts.

Rnd 11: Sc in each sc around, changing to B in last st.

Rnd 12: (2 sc in next sc, sc in next 8 sc) twice—20 sts.

Rnds 20–21: Sc in each sc around, changing to A in last st of Rnd 21.

Rnds 22–23: Sc in each sc around. In last st of Rnd 23, change to B.

Rnds 24–26: Sc in each sc around. In last st of Rnd 26, change to A.

Rnd 27: (Sc2tog, sc in next 8 sc) twice.

Rnd 28: Sc in 18, changing to B in last st.

Rnd 29: (Sc2tog, sc in next 7 sc) twice.

Rnds 30–31: Sc in 16, changing to A in last st of Rnd 31.

Rnd 32: (Sc2tog, sc in next 6 sc) twice.

Rnd 33: Sc in 14, changing to B in last st.

Rnd 32: (Sc2tog, sc in next 5 sc) twice.

Rnds 33–34: Sc in 12. Leaving long tail of each color, fasten off.

Hide beg yarn ends on inside. Use yarn ends from last rnd to attach tail to lower edge of brim.

Boots & Lassos Tunic

● ●

The lassos are created with purchased gold cord that is easy to remove when it is time to launder this bright tunic. The cowboy boots are actually roomy pockets!

Advanced Beginner

MATERIALS

- Reynold's Saucy Sport, 100% cotton (sport weight), 1.75-oz./50g skeins (each 123 yd./112.4m): 8 (10, 11, 13, 14) skeins Red #686 (A), 1 skein Black #899 (B)

- Size 3/D (3.25mm) aluminum crochet hook **or size needed to obtain gauge**

- Tapestry needle

- Hirschberg Schutz, Patch 'Ems Iron-On Appliqués, 1¼ in./3.2cm wide: 4 Gold Stars #AP4823-25

- Gold cord: 2 yd./1.8m

GAUGE

- In Body Pattern: 14 rows and 20 sts = 4 in./10.2cm

- In sc: 14 sts = 3 in./7.6cm 18 rows = 4 in./10.2cm

SIZES

- For girls, 4 (6, 8, 10, 12); directions are written for the smallest size with changes for the larger sizes in parentheses

FINISHED MEASUREMENTS

- Chest: 30 (32, 34, 36½, 39) in./ 76.2 (81.3, 86.4, 92.7, 99.1)cm

- Length: 17 (21, 22½, 24, 25) in./ 43.2 (53.3, 57.2, 61, 63.5)cm

ABBREVIATION

- sc2tog = draw up lp in each of next 2 sts, yo and draw through all 3 lps on hook

Before You Begin

- This tunic is worked from side to side. The row gauge determines the width of the garment, and the stitch gauge determines the length.

- Turn at the end of each row.

BACK

Beg at side, with A, ch 81 (101, 109, 115, 121).

Foundation: Hdc in second ch from hook and in each ch across, ch 15, sl st in first ch; turn—80 (100, 108, 114, 120) sts, not counting ch-lp at end.

Body Pattern: Row 1 (WS): Ch 1, *working in ridge formed by hdc rather than in top of st,* sc in each lp across; turn.

Row 2: Ch 1, hdc in each sc across to end; ch 15, sl st in first ch; turn.

Rep Rows 1 to 2 for Body Pattern for 52 (56, 60, 64, 68) total rows. Fasten off. Piece should measure approx 15 (16, 17, 18¼, 19½) in./38.1 (40.6, 43.2, 46.3, 49.9)cm wide and 16 (20, 21½, 23, 24) in./40.6 (50.8, 54.9, 58.4, 61.0)cm long, excluding ch-lps at lower edge.

FRONT

Work as for Back for 16 (18, 20, 22, 24) total rows, ending with WS row. Fasten off.

Neck Shaping: With RS facing, sk first 9 (10, 11, 12, 13) sts. Join A with sl st in next st. Ch 1, hdc in same sc and in each rem sc across—71 (90, 97, 102, 107) sts; ch 15, sl st in first ch; turn.

Cont est pattern for 19 rows more. On next RS row, ch 10 (11, 12, 13, 14). Hdc in second ch from hook and in each ch across; hdc in each sc across; ch 15, sl st in first ch; turn.

Cont in pattern until 52 (56, 60, 64, 68) total rows have been completed. Fasten off.

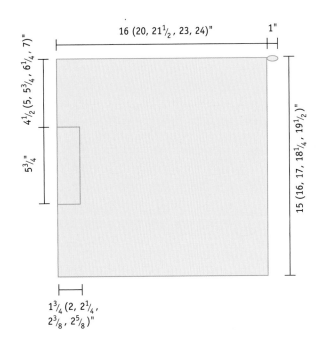

16 (20, 21½, 23, 24)"

1"

4½ (5, 5¾, 6¼, 7)"

5¾"

15 (16, 17, 18¼, 19½)"

1¾ (2, 2¼, 2⅜, 2⅝)"

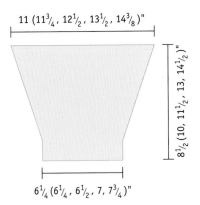

11 (11¾, 12½, 13½, 14⅜)"

8½ (10, 11½, 13, 14½)"

6¼ (6¼, 6½, 7, 7¾)"

SLEEVES (make two)

Beg at lower edge with A, ch 30 (30, 32, 34, 36).

Foundation (RS): Sc in second ch from hook and in each ch across—29 (29, 31, 33, 35) sc. Cont in sc to 2 in. from beg, ending with WS row.

Ch 1, working in front lp only, sc in first sc; * in next sc (sl st, ch 15, sl st), sc in next sc; rep from * across. Ch 1, sc in each rem lp across.

Cont in sc, inc 1 st each edge every other row 9 (10, 10, 8, 7) times then every fourth row 2 (3, 4, 7, 9) times.

Row 7: Sl st in back lp of each sc across and fasten off.

With RS facing and working along opposite edge of Foundation ch, join A with sl st in first ch. Ch 1, sc in same ch as joining and in each of next 6 ch, hdc in next ch, dc in next ch, sk 1 ch, dc in next ch, hdc in next ch, sc in last 7 ch—18 sts.

Rows 2–10: Ch 1, sc in each st across; turn.

Row 11: Ch 1, 2 sc in first sc, sc in each sc across.

Row 12: Ch 1, sc in each sc across, ending 2 sc in last sc.

Rows 13–20: Rep Rows 11 to 12. After Row 20—28 sts.

Row 21: Ch 1, 2 sc in first sc, sc in next 16 sc, sl st in next sc; turn.

Row 22: Ch 1, sk sl st, sc in 17 sc, 2 sc in last sc—19 sts.

Row 23: Ch 1, 2 sc in first sc, sc in 18 sc, sl st in next sc; turn.

Row 24: Ch 1, sk sl st, sc in 19 sc, 2 sc in last sc— 21 sts. Fasten off.

Row 25: With RS facing, join B with sl st in first sc at toe. Ch 1, sc in same sc as join, work 31 more sc across.

Heel: Ch 1, sc in first 7 sc; turn. Ch 1, sc in 7 sc; turn. Sl st in 7 sc, sl st on side of heel, sl st in each sc across, ending in last sc of toe. Fasten off.

Second Boot: Work black Rows 1 to 7 as before; then with WS facing, work first red row. Complete as for first boot.

Turn boots so heels are tog. Mark each boot to indicate RS. With B, straight st in every other row from top of sole to black portion and on the toe side. Using B, straight st in every other row along heel side from top of heel to black portion. Then, overcast with B on each side of straight sts on heel side.

Work even on 51 (55, 59, 63, 67) sts to 8½ (10, 11½, 13, 14½) in./21.6 (25.4, 29.2, 33, 36.9)cm from beg. Fasten off.

BOOTS

With B, ch 20. Sc in second ch from hook and in each of next 8 ch, 3 sc in next ch, sc in last 9 ch; turn.

Row 2 (WS): *Working in back lps for this and each rem black row,* ch 1, sc2tog, sc in 17 sc, sc2tog; turn.

Row 3: Ch 1, sc in 9 sc, 3 sc in next sc, sc in 9 sc; turn.

Rows 4–5: Rep Rows 2 to 3.

Row 6: Rep Row 2.

FINISHING

Stars: Sew one star to each boot center just beneath black top. Place second star with top point three rows down from first star and with side point approx ½ in./1.3cm from front side; sew in place.

Pockets: Position boots onto front of tunic about ¾ in./1.9cm from lower edge and ½ in./1.3cm apart and with toes pointed to sides. Matching colors, sew along lower edge, across back of boot, across top of boot and down to the beg of red front (leave this open for the pocket).

Join shoulder seams. Place markers 6 (6½, 6¾, 7¼, 7¾) in./15.2 (16.5, 17.1, 17.8, 19.7)cm from shoulder seam on each edge. Set in sleeves between markers.

Join underarm and side seams. Then turn back cuffs to row of lps.

Neckband

With RS facing, join A with sl st just to left of the right shoulder seam. Work 22 sl sts across back neck, 8 (9, 10, 11, 12) sl sts along side of neck, 23 sl sts across front neck, and 8 (9, 10, 11, 12) sl sts on rem side of neck.

A Different Look

If you want, make a crocheted chain for the lasso. Use approximately 6 yd. of gold worsted weight yarn to make a chain 2 yd. long. Then slip stitch in the second chain from the hook and in each chain across. Fasten off and knot each end.

Rnd 2: In sl sts of previous rnd, work 31 (32, 33, 34, 35) sc, hdc in next st, sc in next 21 sts, hdc in next st, sc in rem 8 (9, 10, 11, 12) sts.

Rnd 3: Working in front lps, (ch 1, sl st) in each st around for rickrack trim.

Rnd 4: Working in back lps, hdc in each rem lp around.

Rnds 5–10: Rep Rnds 3 and 4.

Rnd 11: Rep Rnd 3.

Rnd 12: Working in back lps, sc in each rem lp around. At end, join with sl st in first sc and fasten off.

Lassos: With A, sew a straight basting line across front bodice ½ in./1.9cm from bottom of armhole. Weave gold cord through raised sts just beneath basting. Form little lassos on each side of center front and big lassos about 2 in./5.1cm from little ones.

Hi Ho! Hi Ho! Off to School We Go

Help your child anticipate the fresh school year
with a new sweater. You'll also find lots of matching surprises
in this section, including purses, doll sweaters,
mittens, and a muffler.

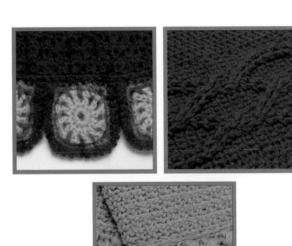

At the Bus Stop

The horizontal cable traveling across the sweater front is actually a long panel with the V-neck top and bottom worked onto it. Thick, warm, and colorful mittens with a long muffler almost cry out for ice skates.

MATERIALS

Sweater

- Dale of Norway Falk Dalegarn, 100% wool (machine-washable, sport weight), 1.75-oz./50g balls (each 116 yd./106m): 11 (12, 14, 15) balls Rust #3727

- Size 5/F (4.00mm) hook **or size needed to obtain gauge**

- Size 6/G (4.25mm) aluminum crochet hook **or size needed to obtain gauge**

Scarf

- Dalegarn Free Style, 100% wool (machine-washable sport weight), 1.75-oz./50g skeins (each 88 yd./80m): 5 skeins Turquoise #6135 (A), 4 skeins Blue #5437 (B), 2 skeins Gold #2427 (C), 2 skeins Orange #3227 (D)

Mittens

- Dalegarn Free Style, 2 skeins Turquoise #6135 (A), 2 skeins Blue #5437 (B), 1 skein Gold #2427 (C), 1 skein Orange #3227 (D)

GAUGE

Sweater

- In Body Pattern with smaller hook: 16 sts and 14 rows = 4 in./10.2cm

- In Cable Pattern with larger hook (see Front): 20 sts = 5 in./12.7cm; 19 rows = 4 in./10.2cm

Scarf

- In double crochet with larger hook: 25 sts = 8 in./20.3cm; 8 rows = 4 in./10.2cm

Mittens

- In single crochet with smaller hook: 17 sts = 4 in./10.2cm; 13 rows = 3 in./7.6cm

- In single crochet with smaller hook and *double strand of yarn*: 13 sts = 4 in./10.2cm; 14 rows = 4 in./10.2cm

SIZES

Sweater

- For boys and girls, 6 (8, 10, 12); directions are written for the smallest size with changes for the larger sizes in parentheses

Scarf

- One size

Mittens

- One size

FINISHED MEASUREMENTS

Sweater

- Chest: 32 (34, 36, 38) in./81.3 (86.4, 91.4, 96.5)cm

- Length: 19 (20, 21, 22) in./48.3 (50.8, 53.3, 55.9)cm

Scarf

- 8 in. by 72 in./20.3cm by 1.8m, excluding fringe

Mittens

- Palm: 7½ in. long by 5 in. wide/19.2cm long by 12.5cm wide

ABBREVIATIONS

- fpdc = front post double crochet: yo, insert hook from front to back then to front to go around dc post, draw up lp, (yo and draw through 2 lps on hook) twice.

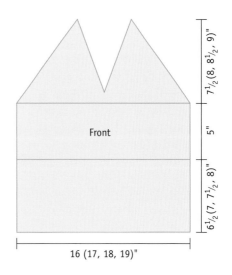

Front

7½ (8, 8½, 9)"

5"

6½ (7, 7½, 8)"

16 (17, 18, 19)"

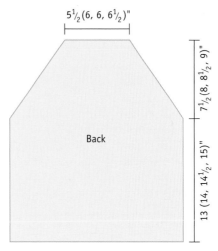

5½ (6, 6, 6½)"

Back

7½ (8, 8½, 9)"

13 (14, 14½, 15)"

2 (2, 2, 2½)"

Sleeve

12½ (13, 14, 15)"

6½ (7, 7½, 8)"

- fpdc over fpdc = on RS, fpdc over fpdc 2 rows below, skipping sc behind new st; on WS, sc in top of fpdc

- bpdc = back post double crochet: yo, insert hook from back to front then to go around dc post, draw up lp, (yo and draw through 2 lps on hook) twice

- hdc2tog = in each of next 2 sts (yo and draw up lp), yo and draw through all 5 lps on hook

- sc2tog = draw up lp in each of next 2 sts, yo and draw through all 3 lps on hook

● ● ● ● ● ● ● ● ● ● ●

Before You Begin

- To change colors in double crochet: With the current color, work the double crochet until two loops remain on the hook; with the next color, yarn over and complete the double crochet.

- To change colors at the end of a row: In the last stitch, draw up a loop with the current color; with the next color, complete the stitch. On the following row, work over both yarn ends for about five stitches to hide them.

- Turn at the end of each row.

PATTERN STITCH
Body Pattern
Row 1: Ch 1, sk first hdc, hdc between first and second hdc; (hdc between next 2 hdc) across; turn.

Rep Row 1 for Body Pattern.

• Sweater •

BACK

Beg at lower edge with smaller hook, ch 65 (69, 73, 77). Hdc in second ch from hook and in each ch across; turn—64 (68, 72, 76) sts. Rep Row 1 of Body Pattern to 11½ (12, 12½, 13) in. from beg.

Raglan Shaping: Working hdc2tog for dec, cont in pattern and dec 1 st each edge now and then every other row 2 (3, 3, 4) times more; then every row 18 (18, 20, 20) times. Cont on rem 22 (24, 24, 26) sts to 19 (20, 21, 22) in./29.2 (30.5, 31.8, 33)cm from beg. Fasten off.

FRONT

Beg at side seam with Foundation for cable panel and using larger hook, ch 21.

Foundation Row: Row 1 (RS): Sc in second ch from hook and each of next 3 ch; (dc in each of next 4 ch, sc in each of next 4 ch) twice—20 sts.

Row 2: Ch 1, sc in each sc and dc across.

Row 3: Ch 1, sc in first 3 sc; * fpdc over next 2 dc, sk 2 sc behind fpdc **, sc in next 2 sc; rep from * across, ending last rep sc in last 3 sc.

Row 4: Ch 1, sc in each sc and fpdc across.

For size 8: Rep Rows 3 to 4 once more. **For size 10:** Rep Rows 3 to 4 twice more. **For size 12:** Rep Rows 3 to 4 for 3 times more.

Cable Panel

Row 1: Ch 1, sc in first 2 sc; (fpdc over fpdc) twice, sk 2 sc behind fpdc. Sc in each of next 4 sc, fpdc over next 4 fpdc and sk 4 sc behind fpdc, sc in next 4 sc, (fpdc over fpdc) twice and sk 2 sc behind fpdcs, sc in last 2 sc.

Row 2 and each WS row: Ch 1, sc in each sc and fpdc across.

Row 3: Ch 1, sc in first 2 sc; fpdc over 2 fpdc and sk 2 sc behind fpdc, sc in 4 sc. (Sk next 2 fpdc, fpdc over third and fourth fpdc, fpdc over first and then second

skipped fpdc—cable made), sk 4 sc behind fpdc, sc in 4 sc, fpdc over 2 fpdc, sk 2 sc behind fpdc, sc in last 2 sc.

Row 5: Rep Row 1.

Row 7: Rep Row 3.

Row 9: Rep Row 1.

Row 11: Ch 1, sc in first 3 sc. * Fpdc over next 2 dc, sk 2 sc behind fpdc **, sc in next 2 sc; rep from * across, ending last rep sc in last 3 sc.

Row 12: Ch 1, sc in each sc and fpdc across.

Row 13: Ch 1, sc in first 4 sc. (Fpdc over next 4 fpdc, sk 4 sc behind fpdc, sc in next 4 sc) twice.

Row 15: Ch 1, sc in first 4 sc. (Cable over next 4 fpdc, and sk 4 sc behind fpdc, sc in next 4 sc) twice.

Row 17: Rep Row 13.

Row 19: Rep Row 15.

Row 21: Rep Row 13.

Row 23: Rep Row 11.

Row 24: Rep Row 2.

Rep Rows 1 to 24 for 2 times more, then rep Rows 1 to 13. **For size 8:** Rep Rows 12 to 13 once again. **For size 10:** Rep Rows 12 to 13 twice more. **For size 12:** Rep Rows 12 to 13 for 3 times more. **For all sizes:** Fasten off.

Size It Right!

The cable panel runs side to side across the front of this sweater. Pay particular attention to the row gauge so that the panel will be the same length as the width of the upper and lower parts of the sweater's front.

Lower Body: With RS facing, using smaller hook, work 64 (68, 72, 76) hdc evenly spaced across one long edge of cable panel. Work Body Pattern to approx 11½ (12, 12½, 13) in./29.2 (30.5, 31.8, 33)cm from beg of the top edge of cable panel. Fasten off.

Upper Body: With RS facing, using smaller hook, work 64 (68, 72, 76) hdc evenly spaced across rem edge of cable panel. Beg Body Pattern, dec 1 st each edge on each of next 3 rows.

Neck Shaping: Ch 1, hdc2tog, work Body Pattern across next 25 (27, 29, 31) sts, hdc2tog; turn.

Left Shoulder: Cont in Body Pattern, shaping raglan as for Back, dec 1 st at neck edge every other row 10 (11, 11, 12) times more. Work even to same length as Back. Fasten off.

Right Shoulder: With RS facing, using smaller hook, sk center st. Join yarn with sl st between center st and next st. Ch 1, hdc2tog over this sp and next sp, work Body Pattern across next 25 (27, 29, 31), hdc2tog; turn. Cont in pattern, shaping raglan and neck as for Left Shoulder.

SLEEVES (make two)

Beg at lower edge, with smaller hook, ch 27 (29, 31, 33). Hdc in second ch from hook and in each ch across—26 (28, 30, 32) sts. Work Body Pattern for 5 more rows. Including new sts into pattern as they

accumulate, inc 1 st each edge every other row 5 (4, 5, 6) times and then every fourth row 7 (8, 8, 8) times more. Work even on 50 (52, 56, 60) sts to 13 (14, 14½, 15) in./33 (35.6, 36.9, 38.1)cm from beg.

Raglan Shaping: Shape raglan as for Back. Work even on rem 8 (8, 8, 10) sts until sleeve measures 21½ (22, 23, 24) in./54.6 (55.9, 58.4, 61)cm from beg. Fasten off.

FINISHING

Using sl st and smaller hook, with WSs tog, join sleeves to front and back. Join underarm and side seams.

Neckband: With RS facing and smaller hook, join yarn with sl st near left back sleeve seam. Ch 1, work 8 (8, 8, 10) sc across top of sleeve, 24 sc along V-neck, 1 sc in center, 24 sc along V-neck, 8 (8, 8, 10) sc across top of sleeve, and 22 (24, 24, 26) sc along back neck. Join with sl st in first sc. Ch 3 (counts as dc); dc in each sc around. At end, join with sl st in third ch of beg ch-3. Fasten off.

• Scarf •

With larger hook and A, ch 27. Dc in fourth ch from hook and in each ch across—25 sts.

Row 2: Ch 3 (counts as dc), dc between first and second sts; (dc between next 2 sts) across.

Row 3: With A rep Row 2, changing to C in last st.

Row 4: With C rep Row 2, changing to B in last st.

Row 5: With B rep Row 2, changing to D in last st.

Rows 6–8: With D rep Row 2. At end of Row 8, change to A.

Rows 9–23: Cont in est pattern working 1 row each of A and C, 3 rows of B, 1 row each of D and A, 3 rows of C, 1 row each of B and D, and 3 rows of A.

Rep Rows 4 to 23 until piece measures approx 30 in./76.2cm from beg. Fasten off.

Make second piece exactly like the first. Matching last turquoise stripes worked from each piece, sew tog.

Fringe: Cut one 11-in./27.9cm long strand of each color. Holding strands tog, fold in half to form lp. With WS facing, take lp through sp bet first and second dc at one end. Draw ends through lp and pull up to form knot. Make fringe for every other sp bet dcs across each end.

• Mittens •

HAND

Cuff: With smaller hook and A, ch 25. Sc in second ch from hook and in each ch across; turn—24 sts. Working sc in back lps for entire cuff, work two more sc rows with A. Then work 1 row of D, 1 row of B, 3 rows of C, 1 row of A, 1 row of D, 3 rows of B, 1 row of C, 1 row of A, 3 rows of D, 1 row of B, 1 row of C, 3 rows of A, 1 row of D, 1 row of B, 3 rows of C, 1 row of A, and 1 row of D. Fasten off.

Palm: With WS of cuff facing (you choose), using smaller hook and *one strand each* of A and B held tog, work 31 sc evenly across one long end of cuff. Work 19 more sc rows. Ch 1, sc2tog, sc in 12 sc, sc2tog, sc in 13 sc, sc2tog. Ch 1, sc across 28 sc. Ch 1, sc2tog across. Ch 1, sc in 14 sc. Ch 1, sc2tog across. Ch 1, sc in 7 sc. Fasten off, leaving tail approx 16 in./40.6cm long.

Thread tail into tapestry needle and take back through front lps of last sc row; pull up to close top. With same tail, join side of palm from top downward, leaving last 3 in./7.6cm of palm free. Secure tail ends on WS. Using either A or D, join cuff seam.

THUMB

With *one strand each* of A and B and smaller hook, join strands at lower edge of opening just above cuff. Ch 1, work 18 sc evenly spaced around opening.

Rnd 2: Sc2tog, sc in 16 sc.

Rnd 3: Sc2tog, sc in 15 sc.

Rnd 4: Sc2tog, sc in 14 sc.

Rnd 5: Sc2tog, sc in 13 sc.

Rnds 6–7: Sc in each of 14 sc.

Rnd 8: Sc2tog around.

Rnd 9: Sc in each of 7 sc. Fasten off, leaving a tail approx 8 in./20.3cm long. Thread tail into needle and take back through front lps of last sc rnd; pull up to close top. Take tail to inside and secure in place.

Fold striped edge toward palm for a 2-in./5.1cm cuff.

Indian Summer Daze

●●●●●●●●●●●●●●●●●●●●●●●●●●

Intermediate

The leaves are changing, and the air is crisp! This vest will add some extra zest over a blouse when a young girl goes shopping for notebooks and pencils. Quickly work up the matching bag, and your girl will be ready for fall! The set is adorable with skirt, shorts, or jeans.

MATERIALS

Vest

- Classic Elite Provence, 100% cotton (sport weight), 4.4-oz./125g hanks (each 256 yd./234m): 1 (2, 2, 2, 2) hanks Lime Green #2681

- Size 4/E (3.5mm) aluminum crochet hook **or size needed to obtain gauge**

- Tapestry needle

Purse

- 1 hank Lime Green #2681

The Set

- 2 (3, 3, 3, 3) hanks Lime Green #2681

GAUGE

- In Body Pattern: 21 sts and 20 rows = 4 in./10.2cm

SIZES

Vest

- For girls, 4 (6, 8, 10, 12); directions are written for the smallest size with changes for the larger sizes in parentheses

Purse

- One size

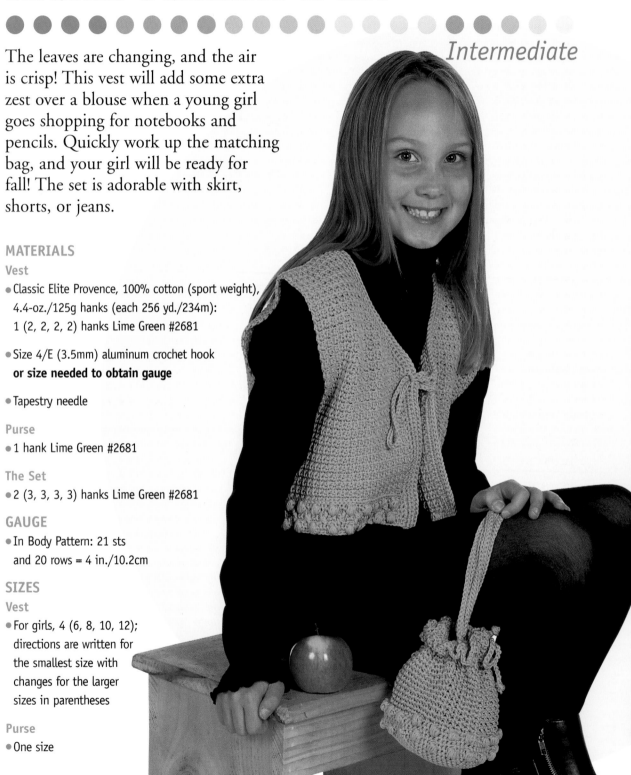

FINISHED MEASUREMENTS

Vest

- Chest (tied): 25½ (28, 29½, 31¾, 33¼) in./64.8 (71.1, 75, 80.6, 84.4)cm

- Length: 8 (9, 11, 12, 13) in./20.3 (22.9, 27.9, 30.5, 33)cm

Purse

- Height: 5½ in./14cm

Before You Begin

- Note that the vest is worked in one piece to the underarm.

- Turn at the end of each row.

PATTERN STITCHES

Puff Stitch

In next st (yo and draw up lp) 5 times, yo and draw through 10 lps on hook, yo and draw through last lp on hook.

BODY PATTERN

multiple of 2 sts + 1 st; rep of 1 row

Row 1: Ch 1, sc in first sc; (ch 1, sk ch-1 sp, sc in next sc) across; turn.

Rep Row 1 for Body Pattern.

• Vest •

BODY

Beg at lower edge, ch 128 (140, 148, 160, 168). Sc in second ch from hook and in each ch across—127 (139, 147, 159, 167) sts; turn.

Border

Row 1 (WS): Ch 1, sc in first 3 sc; * Puff Stitch in next sc, sc in next 3 sc; rep from * across; turn.

Row 2: Ch 1, sc in first 4 sts; * ch 1, sk 1 st, sc in next st; rep from * across, ending sc in last 3 sts; turn.

Row 3: Ch 1, sc in each sc and ch-1 sp across; turn.

Row 4: Ch 1, sc in first 4 sc. * Sk ch-1 sp from Row 2, tr in next ch-1 sp from Row 2, sk 1 sc, sc in next sc, tr in skipped ch-1 sp from Row 2, sk 1 sc, sc in next sc; rep from * across, ending sc in last 3 sc; turn.

Row 5: Rep Row 1.

Row 6: Ch 1, sl st in front lp of each sc across; turn.

Row 7: Ch 1, working in rem lps from Row 6, sc in first lp; (ch 1, sk 1 lp, sc in next lp) across; turn.

Work Body Pattern until piece measures approx 2½ (3, 4½, 5, 5½) in./6.4 (7.6, 11.4, 12.7, 14)cm from beg, ending with WS row.

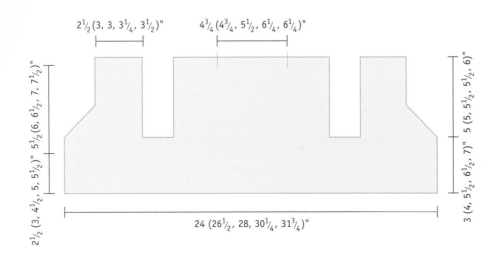

RIGHT FRONT

Ch 1, (sc in sc, ch 1, sk ch-1 sp) across 12 (14, 15, 16, 17) times, sc in next sc—25 (29, 31, 33, 35) sts; turn, leaving rem sts unworked. Cont in Body Pattern until piece measures approx 3 (4, 5½, 6½, 7) in./7.6 (10.2, 14, 16.5, 17.8)cm from beg, ending with RS row.

Neck Shaping: Row 1 (WS): Work est pattern across to last 4 sc, sc in sc, ch 1, sk ch-1 sp, sc in last 2 sc; turn. **Row 2:** Ch 1, sk first sc; work est pattern to end. Rep dec rows until 13 (15, 15, 17, 19) sts rem.

Cont in pattern until piece measures approx 8 (9, 11, 12, 13) in./20.3, 22.9, 27.9, 30.5, 33)cm from beg, ending with RS row. Fasten off.

A Different Look

For a special ocassion, this quick-to-make vest and purse would be great crocheted in white or black to go with a pretty party dress.

BACK

With RS facing, sk 13 sts [(ch-1 sp and sc) 6 times + ch-1 sp]. Join yarn with sl st in next sc. Ch 1, sc in same sc as joining. (Ch 1, sk ch-1 sp, sc in next sc) for 25 (27, 29, 33, 35) times—51 (55, 59, 67, 71) sts; turn, leaving rem sts unworked. Cont est pattern until piece measures approx 8 (9, 11, 12, 13) in./20.3 (22.9, 22.9, 30.5, 33)cm from beg, ending with RS row. Fasten off.

LEFT FRONT

With RS facing, sk 13 sts. Join yarn with sl st in next sc. Ch 1, sc in same sc as joining. (Ch 1, sk ch-1 sp, sc in next sc) for 12 (14, 15, 16, 17) times—25 (29, 31, 33, 35) sts; turn. Complete as for Right Front, reversing neck shaping.

FINISHING

Join shoulder seams.

Front Band

With RS facing, join yarn with sl st in corner of lower right front edge. Ch 1, work 15 (20, 27, 32, 35) sc evenly spaced to V-neck, 3 sc at neck. Work 23 (23, 27,

27, 28) sc evenly spaced to shoulder, 27 (27, 31, 35, 35) sc along back neck, 23 (23, 27, 27, 28) sc evenly spaced to V-neck, 3 sc at neck, and 15 (20, 27, 32, 35) sc evenly spaced to lower edge; turn.

Row 2: Ch 1, sc in 12 (17, 24, 29, 32) sc, ch 3, sk 3 sc, sc in each sc to second corner, sc in 3 sc, ch 3, sk 3 sc, sc in each rem sc to end; turn.

Row 3: Ch 1, sc in each sc around, working 3 sc in each ch-3 sp and 3 sc in each of the two corners. Fasten off.

Row 4: With WS facing, beg at left front band, sl st across band, sl st in each sc around ending sl st across second band. Fasten off.

Tie (make two): With RS facing, join yarn with sl st in center skipped sc of buttonhole. Ch 50. Sl st in top lp of each ch across; sl st in same sc as joining. Fasten off.

Weave loose ends along WS of fabric.

• Purse •

BODY

Beg at base, ch 2. 6 sc in second ch from hook.

Rnd 2: 2 sc in each sc around—12 sts.

Rnd 3: (Sc in sc, 2 sc in next sc) around—18 sts.

Rnd 4: (Sc in 2 sc, 2 sc in next sc) around—24 sts.

Rnd 5: (Sc in 3 sc, 2 sc in next sc) around—30 sts.

Rnd 6: (Sc in 4 sc, 2 sc in next sc) around—36 sts.

Rnd 7: (Sc in 5 sc, 2 sc in next sc) around—42 sts.

Rnd 8: (Sc in 6 sc, 2 sc in next sc) around—48 sts.

Rnd 9: (Sc in 7 sc, 2 sc in next sc) around—54 sts.

Rnd 10: (Sc in 8 sc, 2 sc in next sc) around—60 sts.

Rnd 11: (Sc in 9 sc, 2 sc in next sc) around—66 sts.

Rnd 12: (Sc in 10 sc, 2 sc in next sc) around—72 sts.

Rnd 13 (WS): (Puff Stitch in next sc, sc in next 3 sc) 18 times.

Rnd 14: Sc in each Puff Stitch and sc around.

Rnd 15: Sc in each sc around.

Rnd 16: Rep Rnd 13. At end of rnd, sl st in first sc; turn.

Rnd 17 (RS): (Sc in sc, ch 1, sk 1 st) around.

Rnds 18–31: (Sc in sc, ch 1, sk ch-1 sp) around.

Rnd 32: (Sc in sc, ch 3, sk ch-1 sp) around.

Rnd 33: (Sc in sc, ch 1, sc in ch-3 sp, ch 1) around.

Rnds 34–35: (Sc in sc, ch 1, sk ch-1 sp) around. After Rnd 35; join with sl st in first sc and fasten off.

FINISHING

Strap (make two): With WS facing, join yarn in center skipped sc under a ch-3 lp. Ch 150. Sl st in top lp of each ch across, ending sl st in same sc as joining. Fasten off. Secure ends. Sk 17 ch-3 sps. Make another strap in next sp.

Tie: Ch 100. Sl st in each ch across and fasten off. Weave tie through ch-3 sps so that ends come out between straps. Pull up to close bag. Tie ends into overhand knots. Tie into bow.

Collared Cardigan

●●●●●●●●●●●●●●●●●●●●●●●●●●●●●●●●

Friday night game. Hayride or roller rink. Walking home from her friend's house. She can be "cool" and warm at the same time. Cute with a skirt, dress, or jeans, this jacket in fall colors will become a mainstay.

MATERIALS

Sweater

- Coats & Clark's Aunt Lydia's "Denim," 75% cotton/ 25% acrylic (DK weight), 7.6-oz./215g balls (each 400 yd./365m): 3 (3, 4, 4, 5) balls Linen #1021 (MC), 1 (1, 1, 1, 2) balls Olive #1143 (CC)

- Size 5/F (4.00mm) aluminum crochet hook **or size needed to obtain gauge**

- Tapestry needle

- JHB International Buttons, ¾ in./ 1.9cm in diameter: 5 Ringside #35074 (Green/Ox-Brass)

Bag

- 50 yd./45.7m Olive #1143 (MC), 30 yd./ 27.4m Linen #1021 (CC)

The Set

- 3 (3, 4, 4, 5) balls Linen #1021, 1 (1, 1, 1, 2) balls Olive #1143

GAUGE

- In Body Pattern: 16 sts and 16 rows = 4 in./10.2cm

SIZES

Sweater

- For girls, 4 (6, 8, 10, 12); directions are written for the smallest size with changes for the larger sizes in parentheses

Bag

- One size

FINISHED MEASUREMENTS

- Chest (buttoned): 29¾ (31¼, 33¼, 35¼, 37¾) in./ 75.6 (79.3, 84.4, 90.5, 95.9)cm

- Length: 15 (16, 17, 18½, 20) in./38.1 (40.6, 43.2, 47, 50.8)cm

- Height: 5 in./12.7cm

ABBREVIATIONS

- sc2tog = draw up lp in each of next 2 sts, yo and draw through all 3 lps on hook

●●●●●●●●●●●●

Before You Begin

- Note that the colors in the sweater and bag are reversed: For the sweater, the main color is linen and the contrast color is olive; but for the bag, the main color is olive and the contrast color is linen.

- To decrease in the pattern stitch:

  1. At the beginning or end of a row when there are two single crochets remaining: single crochet two together (sc2tog).

  2. At the beginning of a row when you would normally work a single crochet in the first single crochet, a half double crochet in the next skipped single crochet, and a single crochet in the next single crochet: work a single crochet in the first single crochet, skip the chain-1 space where the half double crochet would have been, and work a single crochet in the next single crochet.

- Each pocket features a snowflake that is worked by following a chart. Read from right to left for right side rows and from left to right for wrong side rows.

- To change colors in single crochet: Draw up a loop with the current color; with the next color, complete the single crochet.

- Turn at the end of each row.

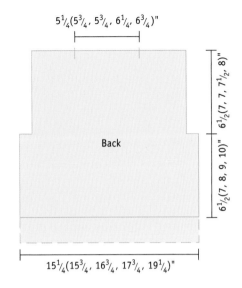

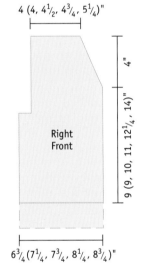

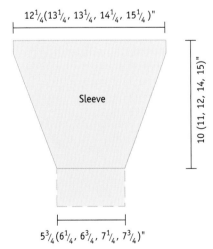

SNOWFLAKE PATTERN

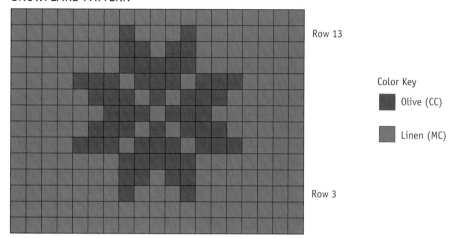

Row 13

Row 3

Color Key

■ Olive (CC)

■ Linen (MC)

PATTERN STITCH
Body Pattern

multiple of 2 sts + 1 st; rep of 4 rows

Row 1 (RS): Ch 1, sc in first sc; (hdc in skipped sc two rows below, sc in sc) across.

Row 2: Ch 1, sc in first sc and hdc; (ch 1, sk sc, sc in hdc) across, ending sc in last sc.

Row 3: Ch 1, sc in first 2 sc; (hdc in skipped sc two rows below, sc in sc) across, ending sc in last sc.

Row 4: Ch 1, sc in first sc; (ch 1, sk 1 sc, sc in hdc) across, ending ch 1, sk 1 sc, sc in last sc.

• Sweater •
BACK

Beg at lower edge with CC, ch 62 (64, 68, 72, 78).

Foundation: With CC, sc in second ch from hook and in each ch across to last ch. In last ch draw up lp with CC, complete the sc with MC—61 (63, 67, 71, 77) sts; fasten off CC.

Next Row: With MC, ch 1, sc in first sc; (ch 1, sk next sc, sc in next sc) across.

Beg Body Pattern and rep Rows 1 to 4 with MC to approx 6½ (7, 8, 9, 10) in./16.5 (17.8, 20.3, 22.9, 25.4)cm from beg, ending with RS row. Fasten off.

Armhole Shaping: With RS facing, join MC with sl st in fifth st from right edge. Ch 1, sc in same st as joining. Rep pattern across, leaving last 4 sts unworked and ending with sc. Cont in pattern on rem 53 (55, 59, 63, 69) sts to approx 13 (14, 15, 16½, 18) in./33 (35.6, 38.1, 41.9, 47)cm from beg. Fasten off.

RIGHT FRONT

Beg at lower edge with CC, ch 28 (30, 32, 34, 36).

Rep Foundation and Next Row as for Back—27 (29, 31, 33, 35) sts. Beg Body Pattern and rep Rows 1 to 4 with MC to approx 6½ (7, 8, 9, 10) in./16.5 (17.8, 20.3, 22.9, 25.4)cm from beg, ending with WS row.

Armhole Shaping: Work in pattern across, leaving last 4 sts unworked—23 (25, 27, 29, 31) sts. Work even to approx 9 (10, 11, 12½, 14) in./22.9 (17.8, 20.3, 22.9, 25.4)cm from beg, ending with WS row.

Neck Shaping: Dec 1 st at neck edge every row 7 (9, 9, 10, 10) times. Work even on rem 16 (16, 18, 19, 21) sts to same length as Back. Fasten off.

LEFT FRONT

Work as for Right Front, reversing Armhole and Neck Shaping.

SLEEVES (make two)

Beg at lower edge, with CC, ch 24 (26, 28, 30, 32). Work Foundation and Next Row as for Back—23 (25, 27, 29, 31) sts.

With MC, rep first 2 rows of Body Pattern. Working 2 sc in first and last sc, cont in pattern across. Including new sts into pattern as they accumulate, inc 1 st each edge every other row 10 (10, 6, 6, 5) times, then inc 1 st each edge every fourth row for 2 (3, 6, 7, 9) times. Cont in pattern on 49 (53, 53, 57, 61) sts to 10 (11, 12, 14, 15) in./25.4 (27.2, 30.5, 35.6, 38.1)cm from beg. Fasten off.

Cuff: With RS facing, join CC in first Foundation ch at lower edge with sl st. Ch 1, sc in same ch as joining and in each ch across—23 (25, 27, 29, 31) sts; join with sl st in beg ch. Without working ch-1 at beg, sc in each sc around and around to approx 2½ in./6.4cm from beg. Fasten off. Fold back cuffs.

POCKETS (make two)

Beg at lower edge with MC, ch 20.

Row 1 (RS): Sc in second ch from hook and in each ch across—19 sts.

Row 2: Ch 1, sc in each sc across.

Rows 3–13: Follow Snowflake Pattern chart. Fasten off CC.

Row 14: With MC, ch 1, sc in each sc across.

Row 15: Ch 1, sl st in front lp of each sc across.

Row 16: Ch 1, sc in each rem lp across.

Rows 17–18: Rep Rows 15 to 16.

Row 19: Rep Row 15. Fasten off.

FINISHING

Join shoulder seams. Set in sleeves, joining sides to skipped armhole sts for square armholes. Join sleeve and side seams.

Lower Band: With CC, sc in each rem lp from Foundation across. Cont in sc to approx 2 in./5.1cm from beg. Fasten off.

Right Front Band

With RS facing, join CC with sl st in lower corner.

Row 1: Ch 1, sc in same sc as join; work 45 (49, 53, 59, 66) additional sc evenly spaced to first V-neck shaping row.

Row 2: Ch 1, sl st in back lp of each sc across.

Row 3: Ch 1, in first rem lp [(sl st, ch 3) count as dc]; dc in each rem lp across.

Row 4: Ch 1, sl st in front lp of each dc across.

Row 5: Ch 1, sl st in each rem lp across. Fasten off.

Left Front Band: With RS facing, join CC with sl st in first V-Neck Shaping row. Rep Right Front Band Rows 1 to 5. Fasten off.

Neckband: With RS facing, join CC with sl st over the dc post near neck edge on right front band. Ch 1, sc in same sp as joining, sc in CC sc; work 17 sc evenly spaced to shoulder, 24 (26, 26, 28, 30) sc across back neck, 17 sc evenly spaced to band, sc in CC sc, sc over dc post. Fasten off.

Collar: With CC, ch 17. Sc in second ch from hook and in each ch across—16 sts. **Row 2:** Working in back lps, ch 1, sc in each sc across. Rep Row 2 for 61 (67, 67, 73, 79) times more.

Before fastening off, place marker at center of top edge of back and at center of long edge of collar. Pin collar in place, matching to edges of front bands. If collar is too small, add rows; if it's too large, subtract rows. When it fits, fasten off. With collar next to WS of sweater body, using CC, sl st in place and fasten off.

Pockets: Center pockets onto fronts, pinning along first MC row. Sew in place.

Button placement: Working along left front band and beg at lower edge, sk first 4 (4, 4, 5, 4) dc; * attach button to next dc, sk next 9 (10, 11, 12, 14) dc; rep from *, placing 5 buttons. Lay sweater on flat surface. Slightly spread sp between top 2 dc on right front band for first buttonhole. Take button through to ensure location. Cont as est until each button has a buttonhole.

Tip for Success

When working with two colors in one row, I usually work over the color not in use as I go along. In this case, however, because the pocket has a light background and a dark motif, I carried the unused strand loosely across the wrong side so that the color would not show through to the right side.

• Bag •

BACK

With MC, ch 19.

Row 1 (RS): Sc in second ch from hook and in each ch across—18 sts.

Row 2: Ch 1, sc in each sc across.

Rep Row 2 for 17 times more.

Eyelet Row: Ch 1, sc in first 7 sc, ch 2, sk 1 sc, sc in next 2 sc, ch 2, sk 1 sc, sc in last 7 sc.

Last Row: Ch 1, sc in each sc and sp across. Fasten off.

FRONT

Work as for Back.

SIDES (make two)

With MC, ch 14. Rep Row 1 as for Back—13 sts. Work 18 more sc rows.

Eyelet Row: Ch 1, sc in first 3 sc, ch 2, sk 1 sc, sc in each of next 5 sc, ch 2, sk 1 sc, sc in last 3 sc.

Rep Last Row as for Back.

BASE

Work as for Back for 12 sc rows.

FLAP

Work as for Back for 7 sc rows.

Buttonhole Row: Ch 1, sc in first 7 sc, ch 4, sk 4 sc, sc in last 7 sc.

Next Row: Ch 1, sc in first sc, (sc2tog) 3 times, 4 sc in ch-4 lp, (sc2tog) 3 times, sc in last sc.

Last Row: Ch 1, sc2tog, sc in each sc across to last 2 sts, sc2tog. Fasten off.

Straps: Join MC with sl st in same st as first trim st. Ch 150. Sl st in same st as joining. Fasten off, leaving tail approx 8 in./20.3cm long. Wrap tail several times around chs near joining, then secure in place on WS. For opposite edge, join MC in same st as last trim st on opposite edge and work as est. Knot top ends tog.

Cord: With double strand of MC, ch 125 and fasten off. Beg with left eyelet on front, take cord from front to back. Weave through rem eyelets, ending at front. Pull ends so they are even. Tie into square knot 3 in./7.6cm from ends; tie into another square knot. Tie square knots at ch ends. The double knot forms the "button."

FINISHING

Cut two 54-in./1.4m strands of CC. Holding strands tog, thread into tapestry needle. Working from bottom to top, weave through rows at left edge of one side; then weave through rows at right edge of front from top to bottom. With same strand, insert needle from inside and under first CC st on side, pull strand through; then, insert needle from inside and under first CC st on front and pull strand through; rep to top. Secure ends on WS of fabric. Join second side to opposite edge of front, and then join back to sides. For base, cut two 4-yd./3.6m strands of CC, and join Base to all four sides at bottom of bag. Join flap to back of bag as est.

Trim: With RS facing, join double strand of CC to right edge of flap with sl st. Ch 1, sc in same sp as joining. Work 29 more sc evenly spaced around. Fasten off.

"In Crowd" Standout

● ●

Brushed acrylic yarn in a girl's favorite colors
combined with easy stitches make this cape
a treasure. As a surprise gift, what little gal
would not be pleased?

Intermediate

MATERIALS

- Lion Brand Imagine, Art, 80% acrylic/20% mohair
  (worsted weight, #780) 2.5-oz./71g per solid
  skein (each 222 yd./203m) and 2-oz./57g
  per multicolor skein (each 179 yd./163.6m):
  3 (4, 4, 5) skeins Purple Haze #338 (MC),
  1 skein Maize #186 (A), 1 skein Autumn
  Leaves #325 (B)

- Size 6/G (4.25mm) aluminum
  crochet hook **or size needed
  to obtain gauge**

- Yarn needle

GAUGE

- Rnds 1–4 of Granny
  Square = 2½ in./
  6.4cm square

- In Body Pattern: 10 V-sts = 6 in./
  15.2cm; 13 rows = 4 in./10.2cm

SIZES

- For girls, 6 (8, 10, 12); directions are written
  for the smallest size with changes for the larger
  sizes in parentheses

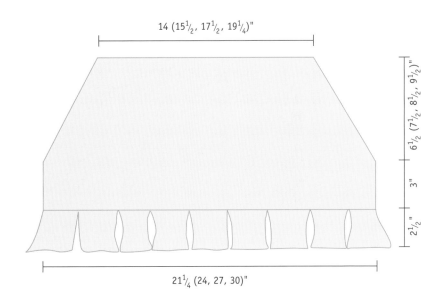

14 (15½, 17½, 19¼)"

6½ (7½, 8½, 9½)"

3"

2½"

21¼ (24, 27, 30)"

FINISHED MEASUREMENTS
- Chest: 28 (31, 35, 38½) in./71.1 (78.7, 88.9, 97.8)cm
- Lower Edge: 42½ (48, 54, 60) in./108 (121.9, 137.2, 152.4)cm
- Length: 13 (14, 15, 16) in./33 (35.6, 38.1, 40.6)cm

ABBREVIATION
- V-st = (hdc, ch 1, hdc) in next sc

●●●●●●●●●●●●

Before You Begin
- The first step to making this cape is to crochet all the Granny Squares.
- Turn at the end of each row.

PATTERN STITCH
Granny Square
With A, ch 2.

Rnd 1 (RS): 12 sc in second ch from hook; join with sl st in first sc.

Rnd 2: Ch 4 (counts as dc, ch-1); (dc, ch 1) in each sc around. Join with sl st in third ch of beg ch-4. Fasten off.

Rnd 3: With the RS facing, join B with sl st in any ch-1 sp. Ch 1, sc in same sp as joining. (Ch 2, sc in next ch-1 sp) around, ending ch 2, sl st in first sc.

Rnd 4: Ch 1; * 2 sc in each of next 2 ch-2 sps, 5 sc in next sp; rep from * around 4 times. At end, join in first sc and fasten off.

Body Pattern
multiple of 10 on RS rows; multiple of 10 + 1 on WS rows; rep of 2 rows

Row 1 (RS): Ch 1, hdc in first sc; * sk 1 sc, V-st in next sc; rep from * across, ending sk 1 sc, hdc in last sc; turn.

Row 2: Ch 1, sc in first hdc, sc before next hdc; (sc bet next 2 hdc) across, ending sc in last hdc; turn.

Rep Rows 1 to 2 for Body Pattern.

GRANNY SQUARES
Make 14 (16, 18, 20) Granny Squares.

BACK
With RS facing and MC, work 10 sc across each of 7 (8, 9, 10) Granny Squares—70 (80, 90, 100) sts; turn. Sl st in back lp of each sc across; turn. Ch 1, working in rem lps, sc in each lp across, inc 1 st in center—71 (81, 91, 101) sts. Fasten off.

With RS facing, join MC with sl st in first sc and beg Body Pattern with Row 1—70 (80, 90, 100) sts. Cont in pattern until piece measures approx 5½ in./14cm from beg, ending with WS row.

Shaping: Row 1 (RS): Ch 1, hdc in first sc, sk 1 sc, hdc in next sc; (sk 1 sc, V-st in next sc) across, ending (sk 1 sc, hdc in next sc) twice—68 (78, 88, 98) sts; turn. **Row 2:** Ch 1, sc in first hdc, sk 1 hdc; (sc between next 2 hdc) across, ending sk 1 hdc, sc in last hdc; turn.

Cont in Body Pattern, rep Shaping Rows 1 to 2 every fourth row 2 (2, 3, 5) times and then every other row 3 (4, 4, 3) times. Work even on rem 46 (52, 58, 64) sts for RS rows to approx 12 (13, 14, 15) in./ 30.5 (33, 35.6, 38.1)cm from beg, ending with WS row. Fasten off.

FRONT

Work as for Back.

FINISHING

Join side seams.

Turtleneck: With RS facing, join MC with sl st in sc next to side seam. **Rnd 1:** Ch 1, hdc in same sc as joining; * sk next sc, hdc in next sc; rep from * around, ending sk next sc—46 (52, 58, 64) sts. Place marker to indicate beg of rnd. Work 13 more hdc rnds. Fasten off. Let turtleneck roll to outside.

Neck Trim: Holding cape upside down and with RS facing, *using one strand each* of A and B held tog, join with sl st around first hdc from Rnd 1. (Ch 3, sl st over next hdc) around, ending ch 3, sl st in same hdc as joining. Fasten off.

Cut 2½ in./6.4cm lengths of A and B. Alternating so that one fringe has 2 A and 1 B and next fringe has 2 B and 1 A, hold 3 strands tog. With cape upside down, fold strands in half to form lp. Take lp under a ch-3, draw ends through lp and pull up to form knot. Cont adding fringe to each ch-3 sp around. Trim ends.

Lower Edging: With RS facing, join MC in top sc at side edge of one Granny Square near side seam of cape. (Ch 1, sl st in next sc) around each square for rickrack edging. At end, fasten off.

Tip for Success

Wrap one strand each of the fringe colors loosely around your hand about 50 times. Cut one side of lps. Now, you can easily divide up the strands for the fringe.

RESOURCES

MANUFACTURERS

The following companies sell wholesale only. Contact them to locate retail stores in your area.

Berroco, Inc.
14 Elmdale Rd.
P.O. Box 367
Uxbridge, MA 01569-0367
(508) 278-2527
www.berroco.com

Classic Elite Yarns
300 Jackson St.
Lowell, MA 01852
(978) 453-2837

Coats & Clark
8 Shelter Dr.
Greer, SC 29650
(800) 648-1479
www.coatsandclark.com

Dale of Norway, Inc.
N16W23390 Stoneridge Dr.,
Ste. A
Waukesha, WI 53188
(262) 544-1996
www.dale.no

Elmore-Pisgah, Inc.
204 Oak St.
P.O. Box 187
Spindale, NC 28160
(704) 286-3665
www.elmore-pisgah.com

JCA, Inc.
35 Scales Ln.
Townsend, MA 01469
(978) 597-8794

JHB International, Inc.
1955 S. Quince St.
Denver, CO 80231
(303) 751-8100
www.buttons.com

Knit One, Crochet Too!
2220 Eastman Ave. #105
Ventura, CA 93003-7794
(805) 676-1176

Lion Brand Yarn Co.
34 W. Fifteenth St.
New York, NY 10011
(212) 243-8995
www.lionbrand.com

Spinrite, Inc.
320 Livingstone Ave. South
P.O. Box 40
Listowel, ON
Canada N4W 3H3
(519) 291-3780
www.spinriteyarns.com

S. R. Kertzer Ltd.
105A Winges Rd.
Woodbridge, ON
Canada L4L 6C2
(905) 856-3447
www.kertzer.com

The Plymouth Yarn Co., Inc.
500 Lafayette St.
P.O. Box 28
Bristol, PA 19007
(215) 788-0459
www.pymouthyarn.com

MAIL-ORDER AND WORLD WIDE WEB SOURCES

eKnitting.com
1625 University Ave.
Berkeley, CA 94703
(800) 392-6494
www.eKnitting.com

Herrschners' Yarn Shoppe
2800 Hoover Rd.
Stevens Point, WI 54492-0001
(800) 441-0838
www.herrschners.com

**Mary Maxim Needlework
and Crafts**
2001 Holland Ave.
P.O. Box 5019
Port Huron, MI 48061-5019
(800) 962-9504
www.marymaxim.com

Patternworks
P.O. Box 1690
Poughkeepsie, NY 12601
(800) 438-5464
www.patternworks.com

The Wool Connection
34 E. Main St.
Old Avon Village North
Avon, CT 06001
(800) 933-9665
www.woolconnection.com

Yarn Barn of Kansas
930 Massachusetts
P.O. Box 334
Lawrence, KS 66044
(800) 468-0035
www.yarnbarn-ks.com